Be Wise Small

To The Simmers with love,

Be Wise Small
A Lifetime of Distilled Wisdom

Dee Bowman

ISBN: 978-0-89098-912-8

©2016 by 21st Century Christian

2809 12th Ave S, Nashville, TN 37204

All rights reserved.

All rights reserved. No part of this publication may be reproduced, stored in a retrieval system, or transmitted in any form or by any means—electronic, mechanical, photocopy, recording, digital, or otherwise—without the written permission of the publisher.

Cover design and layout by Marc Hinds (www.HindsDesign.com)
with Jonathan Edelhuber

To my Norma

Foreword

With the advent of electronic reading, namely through Amazon's wonderful Kindle e-reader, it didn't take long for us to realize the potential of a monthly "brotherhood paper" for e-readers. Careful talk, planning and prayer led to the creation of an electronic journal, *Pressing On*.

Yet while it may have seemed that our agenda was to get quality, scriptural material on to people's electronic devices, there was something else going on. We hope to escape charges of being nefarious, but in truth, we saw *Pressing On* as a way to re-activate one of the most powerful pens among us today. In simple terms, we wanted Dee Bowman to write again.

In the early 1980s his magnificent, practical writings in his column "That's Life" had been a highlight of *Christianity Magazine*'s monthly appearances. He made us laugh, he made us cry, he introduced us to brethren we should know, and over and over, he challenged us to live as true disciples should.

Dee had written for various publications through the years since CM had ceased publication, but had not done a regular column again. Thus, the first columnist we approached about writing was Dee Bowman. We knew his writing would bless people like no one else's. We knew brethren would appreciate him writing again. And, quite frankly, we ourselves wanted to read from his pen again. He has a unique ability to use the Word of God to understand and anticipate our need. Then, to address that need from the same Source. He matches concepts with conduct, because he loves people.

It is a joy then to introduce this collection of his columns, thoughts, and ideas that are just quintessentially "Dee." Dee has always urged us to live a life that gets the details right, that honors the Lord even in the minor matters. "Be Wise Small" constantly and consistently keeps us on that track. We are convinced by our experience with Dee Bowman, this book will take you to sound biblical perspectives which will serve you well. Dee uses his wit and way with words to storm the will of his readers, based on the revealed wisdom of God.

We hope and pray that you will enjoy Dee's writings as we have, and that these things will help you press on in your walk with Christ Jesus.

Mark Roberts, editor
Warren Berkley, assistant editor

Introduction

Excuse my intrusion, but I have a small suggestion. It's simple, to the point, and not difficult to follow, and yet it seems to me to be needed in every person's life.

"Be wise small" may sound a bit off-key, but don't be fooled by its simplicity. It's actually a big part of life. It's an attribute and attitude that should be started early and then practiced in every area of life.

I used to make several New Years resolutions every January—then promptly break most of them before the first month was out. But then I came up with one simple resolution. It was to "be wise small." Now after several years, I'm still working on that same simple little resolution. It's been an interesting and profitable journey. It has stood me in good stead, so I thought I would pass it on to you. I hope it helps you. It has helped me.

It's actually rather simple. What you try to do is be wise about even the smallest matters. If you miss the trash can, you go and pick it up. Better still, if you notice that someone else has missed the trash can, you go and pick their miss. You take the grocery cart to the proper place, even if it was someone else who left it out. And you do it even when nobody's looking.

I concluded that if you continue to be wise about even the smallest matters you will soon develop a habit, then when the time comes, you will be wise about the large matters, almost habitually. And so—*Be Wise Small*.

Be Wise Small is not intended to have a thematic woven into it. It has no special subject to which it returns. Rather, it is intentionally dis-connected, desultory. The reason is simple. It is written so that you can open it at any page, point your finger at any entry, and find something there to contemplate and muse, even for just a few minutes. It has simple little bits and pieces which are intended to make their way to the back porch, or the sun room, or wherever you can spend a few minutes musing and contemplating spiritual matters.

Most of this work first appeared in the e-magazine *Pressing On*, edited by Mark Roberts and co-edited by Warren Berkley, personal friends and fellow-laborers of mine. I am indebted to both these fine men for their invitation to write for their periodical and for the personal encouragement both men have given me through the years. And thanks too, to Tom Tignor of 21st Century Christian who made valuable suggestions to ready the work for publication. He saw what I had in mind.

And special thanks to Paul Earnhart, Ed Harrell, Sewell Hall, and Brent Lewis, who tolerated my "That's Life" column for all those years; and to the Southside congregation in Pasadena, Texas, who tolerated my oblique schedule for over 40 years. And special appreciation to Bubba Garner with whom I have shared the pulpit for nearly 20 years.

Be Wise Small
A Lifetime of Distilled Wisdom

Things My Daddy Told Me

My dad was king of the roost around our house. The scepter of his authority was a big, black razor strop. It hung on the wall behind the bathroom door. He knew how and when to wield it. Just the sign of it brought horror to the soul. Now, he never misused it, but he was not afraid to use it when the occasion called for it. He would always say just before he administered the punitive measures, "this hurts me more than it hurts you." I never understood that. The seat of his pants weren't on fire.

One day he called me and my brothers—all four of us—and said, "You boys get outside and line up, I'm going to give you all a spanking." "Why, Dad, what did we do?" "Just on general principles," he said, "I know you've done something or other wrong today, so I'm just gonna spank you." He lined us up, scared us good, popping that black thing back and forth, and then suddenly went back into the house laughing. He made his point.

> **"This hurts me more than it hurts you." I never understood that.**

The things my daddy told me have stood me in good stead through the years. He was a Christian. He had a good grasp of what was wise and what was not, even the little stuff. Here are some things my Daddy told me (and some things My Heavenly Father tells me):

- "Listen to Me" (Proverbs 3:5–6; 4:13; James 1:19)
- "Stand up straight (Ephesians 6: 11, 13, 14)
- "Watch where you're going (Matthew 7:13–14; Psalm 119:104–105)
- "Be careful what you let in (Ephesians 4:27; Luke 8:18)
- "Think about it before you do it" (Proverbs 23:7; 2 Corinthians 10:3–5; Philippians 4:8)
- "Watch your mouth" (Psalm 141:3; Proverbs 13:3; Ephesians 4:29; Colossians 4:6; James 3:1–12)
- "Know why" (1 Peter 4:11; Romans 13:10; 15:1–6)
- "Take out the trash" (Philippians 3:4–11; Colossians 3:8–10; James 1:21; Romans 13:10–14)
- "Remember who you are" (1 Peter 2:9–11; 4:11)

Small Thoughts I Had Today

Some people can't give a compliment or word of encouragement, assuming that to do so diminishes in some way from their own personal worth.

Talent very often breeds criticism.

Sincerity is usually stronger than force.

Accord is like a chord—just get a little out of tune and there will invariably be discord.

Moral strength is apt to be measured as much by longevity as by a sudden burst of power.

Sometimes it takes more courage to resist speaking than to speak.

A Lifetime of Distilled Wisdom

You can't say something to somebody without showing somewhat how you feel about the matter.

Indifference is one of the main enemies of truth.

The best medicine for depression is to go out and do something for somebody.

You may get all the way to third base, but it doesn't count until you score.

From Other Sources

"The only thing needed for evil to succeed is for good men to do nothing."
—*Sir Edmund Burke*

"Unless the measuring rod is independent of the thing measured, we can do no measuring."
—*C. S. Lewis*

"There's no use in doing a kindness if you do it a day too late."
—*Charles Kingsley*

Give Thanks Today...

- ▶ for someone who loves you.
- ▶ for the little things in life.
- ▶ for the times in which we live.
- ▶ for the privilege of approaching your Father.
- ▶ for the possibility of forgiveness.

Hold Hands

I was thinking awhile back about some simple small, but wise things that can help hold a marriage together. You know what I came up with? When we were dating we held hands. Why did we stop?

- Hold hands when you pray—at worship services, too.
- Hold hands when you see some special scene.
- Hold hands when you're mad.
- Hold hands when you're sad.
- Hold hands when you walk from the car to the grocery store.
- Hold hands when you see the little one sleeping.
- Hold hands when you laugh.
- Hold hands when you cry.
- Hold hands as you walk along life's pathway together.

If you're not doing it—start today. It'll make things better. Just hold hands.

Be Careful!

Here's a quick look at Proverbs 13:1–5 that I call "Be Careful!" It's "be wise small" stuff.

Verse 1—Listen up! That's where being careful begins. You can't catch on if you don't tune in.

Verse 2—Be careful or you may have to eat your words. The aftertaste is awful.

Verse 3—Be careful not to open your mouth too wide. It's easy to put your foot in it if you do.

Verse 4—Be careful what you want. If all you want is nothing, that's what you're apt to get.

Verse 5—Be careful with the truth. Even truth can be turned in the wrong way if you do stuff to it.

Short Stops

Peace is not so much the absence of war as just knowing you're right with God.

When Helen Keller came to understand about God, she is reported to have said, "I knew he was there, I just didn't know what to call him."

Sometimes a little subtraction can add a lot to the situation.

If we gave as much thought to giving as we do to getting, what a different world it would be.

Some Thoughts From My Journal

If you get in too big a hurry, you're more apt to stumble.

The better you get at what you do, the more criticism you're apt to get.

Sincerity and simplicity are first cousins.

The more you get, the more you won't.

Living the Christian life is a constant course-correcting maneuver. It's all about trying to keep your vehicle between the ditches.

Kermit the frog sings, "It's not easy being green." And it's not. We have to keep trying.

Just a Little

- "A little leaven leavens the whole lump" (1 Corinthians 5:6)
- "A little sleep, a little slumber, a little folding of the hands..." (Proverbs 6:9–10)
- "Oh, ye of little faith" (Matthew 6:30)
- "Life is a vapor that appeareth for a little while..." (James 4:10)
- "Four things that are little on the earth..." (Proverbs 30:24)

A Small Sermon

I have sought in vain to find an etymological connection between the word *responsibility* and the concept, *response to ability*. There is none. But the conceptual connection is certainly there. One who is responsible is one who must respond to his ability. Everyone has ability and everyone has to respond to that ability. That adds up to responsibility. The Scriptures are replete with calls for proper use of talent and ability. "Work out your own salvation with fear and trembling" (Philippians 2:12) is a good example. That leave anybody out? How're you doing with yours?

> **One who is responsible is one who must respond to his ability.**

Small Pieces

How can we speak of "laws of nature," if there is no lawgiver.

I once heard Jack L. Holt ask, "If there was a big bang, where is the big banger?"

Moods are like cold fronts. If they stall, they usually bring trouble.

One small controversy can rupture in minutes a relationship that was years in the making.

I don't care how hard you have to try, if it's any good, it's worth it.

If you can't thank God for it, you better not do it!

Be Wise Small—But Watch Out!

I wrote this in my journal awhile back. "Not as many people are kind in today's world. I'm not sure why. Even when you act in a kind manner toward someone, they look perplexed, as if you have some ulterior motive or something." Be kind anyway. Be kind small. But be careful. I opened the door for a lady recently and was promptly told she didn't need any help from me—after which I got a women's-lib lecture.

A Little More

Be sure you're going the right way, then give it all you've got (John 6:68).

If it's better felt than told, it might not be better (Psalm 119:11).

If you have to look around to see if someone is looking before you do it, it might be a good idea to stop and think about what you're about to do (Proverbs 5:1–2).

Mr. Jackson knew the Scriptures. He would defend the truth when he was downtown where he whittled away the time whittling on a stick and talking to his buddies down at the city square. "I don't understand why old Mr. Jackson doesn't obey the gospel," I said to my Dad. "Simple, son," he said, "he's never repented." Simple.

Your Own Back Yard

I don't have a very big backyard (great for mowing), but I like being out there. I have an office out there. I like to go out and listen to my music, meditate a bit. And I love to sit on the patio and watch the birds. They scamper around the feeder, fly away in a flush, and then, one by one, come back until there's a big crowd again. It's just kinda nice to hang around your own back yard.

Your own back yard...

- Is a good place to be yourself (the Lord knows the real you, anyhow).
- Is a good place for growing things (including good thoughts, good plans, and stuff).
- Is a good place for fencing off the world (so you let God into your life for a little while).
- Is a good place to hear the birds (and the sound of your own heart).
- Is a good place to make plans to improve your yard (and yourself).
- Is a good place to repair your fence if it needs it (and your life, if it needs it).
- How long since you've been out there?

Silent Speech

There's such a thing, I think, as *silent speech*. We can say things without ever saying a word. Don't we often say, "that says something about him" when not a word was uttered? May I suggest some things you can say without a podium or a soapbox?

Say something to others by how you speak. If you speak with a clean tongue at all times and on all matters, you say something about yourself. A filthy mouth bespeaks a foolish heart.

Say something to others by what you wear. Sloppy dress suggests something about you. Provocative clothing says something, too. And so does proper attire. Clothing speaks.

Say something to others by how you act. Everybody wants a good time, but when fun goes ballistic and restraint goes out the window, it speaks volumes about who and what you are.

Say something to others by your choice of associates. Stay long enough with the wrong people and you'll become like them. Stay with good folks and you'll be influenced by their good manners. Who you're with speaks considerably to what you've chosen to be.

Say something to others by where you go. If you go places where evil is king, it says you don't care. If you're the only one on your block who attends worship services on Lord's Day, it says to your neighbors that you want to worship Him, to recommend Him, to follow Him. If you don't ever attend it says you're like everybody else—you don't care to be there.

Need I say more? Just be wise small.

From My Journal

It is impossible, I aver, to measure the grace of God. It reaches to the very depth of man's need and the height of God's own glory.

Never is God's grace more brilliantly displayed than in His patience. It is indefatigable, inexhaustible . That He would actually "wait that He might be gracious" (Isaiah 30:18) is illustrative of how great is His grace.

Without such patience we would have no hope, but with such waiting, we will one day have the opportunity to exalt His wonderful name in glory. Amazing Grace!

Short Stops
What you do in life is do with what you have to do with—or something like that.

The best map is no good unless somewhere on it there is a notation that says "you are here." Compare God's Word.

The ancient, original sense of the word "good" was "to bring together, to unite." Look what that does to the statement "God is good."

Are you aware that there's an etymological connection between the word *attitude* and the word *aptitude?* It makes sense when you think about it, because your *attitude* is what you're *apt* to do.

Just a little bit of Scripture can sometimes open the door to a good bit of discussion.

Leftovers
Sometimes I write late at night—whether I want to or not.

Life is sweet, sometimes sour; sometimes it changes within the hour.

I Was Just Thinking...
You can't be truly happy until you view yourself as having little value when divorced from a relationship with your Father.

You won't be truly happy unless you become sincerely devastated about sin and unrighteousness—yours or other's.

You won't be truly happy until you have put reins on yourself and know when to get angry and when not to.

You won't be truly happy until you love truth so much that you can't wait to learn more of it.

You won't be truly happy until you have learned how to extend to others the same loving kindness you expect from them.

You won't be truly happy until you develop a heart that is devoid of any rancor or other kinds of impure thoughts.

You won't be truly happy until you consider it your responsibility—even your pleasure—to pursue and promote peace everywhere you can.

You won't be truly happy until your regard for truth and piety is so intense that you will be willing—even glad—to suffer for it.

Hey, wait a minute! I think I just did the beatitudes.

Some Great Men of God

- **Abraham**—because of his faith.
- **Joseph**—because of his virtue.
- **Solomon**—because of his wisdom.
- **David**—because of his love for God's Word.
- **Moses**—because of his meekness.
- **John the Baptist**—because of his humility.
- **Peter**—because of His courage.
- **John**—because of his love.
- **Paul**—because of his devotion.
- But most of all **Jesus**, because He was all of these and so much more.

Some Thoughts on Colossians 1:9–11

William George Jordon wisely said, "Life is not a competition with others. In its truest sense it is a rivalry with ourselves.

- ▶ I must live up to my own possibilities (vs. 9).
- ▶ I must make today better than yesterday (vs. 9).
- ▶ I must improve what I have that is useful (vs. 10).
- ▶ I must learn to diminish the effect of some nagging weakness I drag around (vs. 11)
- ▶ I must be evermore grateful for what I have been given of God (vs. 12).

My Heroes

I guess we all have had our heroes. I love baseball. Lou Bodreau, the Cleveland Indians' shortstop, was my hero when I was a kid—still is, I guess. I've always loved the Four Freshmen. Still keep in touch with one of the originals, Ross Barbour. But could I tell you about another one of my heroes?

A young girl in Alabama handed me a note the last night of the meeting. It said, "I know it's got to come from the heart, and I have to change for myself. I've done so many things I now regret, but Tuesday night after the sermon, I went home and poured out my heart to God. Please keep me in your prayers—even after you leave." (Enclosed was a ten dollar bill.) "I know this is not much," she said, "but maybe it'll help you some. I love you" Signed, "Jeannie."

Jeannie's one of my all-time heroes.

Ten Short Paragraphs for Your Marriage

Have time for one another. Being alone with one another—even for just a few minutes—keeps you in touch, gives you a chance to listen to one another, keeps the lines of communication open. Lots of times, you just need to get away from the pressing duties of daily living and stay acquainted.

Be careful what you say and how you say it. Just because you're married doesn't give you the right to say whatever you want or say something just however you want to say it. Bad words pile up. And they can be explosive at times. Sometimes it's not so much what you say, but how you say it that makes the difference.

Understand the true meaning of subjection. Whether you're the husband or the wife, you have to understand what subjection is in marriage. It's doesn't give the husband the right to be dictatorial, and it doesn't call for the wife to be cowered and huddled in fear all the time. God's manner of subjection produces a balanced marriage, one where both parties are carefully submissive to their role in the relationship. Understanding subjection helps.

> **Learn to be mad short.**

Manifest your love in more than one way. Sex is certainly a statement of love, but it's not the only way to say it. An unexpected gift. A card on the pillow. A text message, "just to say I'm thinking about you." Little stuff like that makes marriage fun, keeps it active, and makes it stable.

Learn how to have a fuss. Fusses are part of marriage. And if they're handled right, they can have a useful purpose. They tend to clear the air. They can make points of emphasis clear, and bring little gripes to the surface. But they have to be short to accomplish that. So be careful—learn to be mad short.

Learn the joy of tolerating one another's warts. Everybody has them, you know—even you. Develop a sense of humor about one another's nagging little idiosyncracies. There's a kind of satisfaction in having enough love for someone to overlook the little stuff they do or don't do, or how they say things, or how they rub their nose, or something. We all have warts. True love looks the other way and grins.

Don't let the kids dominate your life. Undue attention to children can have a bad effect on a marriage. You'll have the kids with you for about twenty years or so, but your mate will still be there when they're gone. So be sure to take care of your relationship with your guy or your gal while you're rearing your children. Marriage is for life, and having a good marriage means knowing when to emphasize what.

Find friends. Good friends make marriages stronger. They're there in the good times, so we laugh together. And they're there when things are not so good, so we cry together. They become a part of who and what we are. Good friends make the times in marraige what it ought to be.

Expect trouble. There will be times of sadness and sorrow in your marriage, so don't be surprised when those times come. Bad things and sad things will happen, but love will always out. Love is the divine foundation. It will sustain the relationship even when the hardest times come. So love one another, lean on one another, help one another. Trials, when they are handled properly, tend to strengthen a marriage and make it strong. Whatever comes, remember that God is on His throne and that you love one another. You can make it, if you love Him and love one another.

Keep God first in your marriage. Pray together. Cry together. Be happy together. Be sad together. Raise kids together. Even fuss a little. Then sit down and thank God for every bit of it. After all, He gave you the whole lovely thing.

After you're done with this, sit down and read 1 Corinthians 13 and see if all these things aren't in that passage.

A Small Prayer

O Father, give me wisdom that I may not say more than need be said.

Part-Time Christians

A part-time Christian attends part of the time.

A part-time Christian has a half-hearted dedication.

A part-time Christian has a part-time prayer life.

A part-time Christian controls his tongue—part of the time.

A part-time Christian denies "faith only," but practices it part of the time.

A part-time Christian has a part-time devotion to spirituality.

Suppose there will be a place in heaven for part-time Christians?

Little Things Mean a Lot

A little love can go a long, long way.

A little encouragement can help someone get where he's going.

A little care can be the beginning of a lot of care.

A little listening can help a friend endure.

A little wisdom can be at least a little benefit.

A Few Pertinent Questions

How much did you pray today?

Did you speak up when you should have?

How is your spiritual life? Are you growing?

What dominated your thinking today?

If today were the last day of your life, would you be satisfied with it?

Be Wise Small-isms

A foolish man is always looking to tomorrow; a wise man takes care of today first.

There is likely no greater waste than the waste of time.

"Progress always involves risks. You can't steal second base and keep your foot on first."
—Frederick B. Wilcox

And could I add this? You don't score just because you got to third.

A hope realized just means there's still more to do.

"Opportunity" is a from a nautical term meaning a favorable port. Tell you anything?

Even the pretty people get old—if they live long enough.

"Human happiness and moral duty are inseparably connected."
—George Washington

What Ever Happened?

    To family meals?

    To bedtime stories for children?

    To just dad and son playing ball?

    To just mom and daughter sewing?

    To families sitting together at services?

Reckon where all that went?

Concern For Concern

Life is not a competition with others. In its truest since, it is a rivalry with ourselves. I'm not sure where I first read that, but I think it certainly to be true.

We live in a world of cultural contradictions:

- ▶ We're more concerned with how we look than how we are.
- ▶ We're more concerned with what people think than what God knows.
- ▶ We're more concerned with who we are than what we are.
- ▶ We're more concerned about getting than with giving.
- ▶ We're more concerned with the here and now than with the hereafter.

"Examine Yourself" (2 Corinthians 13:5)

- ▶ That's hard.
- ▶ It takes a standard from which to commence, one greater than yourself.
- ▶ It takes personal integrity.
- ▶ It takes careful concentration.
- ▶ It takes a sincere dedication to truth.
- ▶ It takes a steady continuance.
- ▶ That's hard.

Small Stuff From a Fellow's Journal

"I'm ready to go home, though. No matter who you see or what, there's no place like home. That's more of a truism than a cliché. It's great to go; greater to come home. I guess that's how it will be at the end as well."

> **The providence of God is a fact confirmed in Scripture.**

"Man would never have known God for Who and What He is separate from inspiration. Had He not seen fit to make Himself known, we would be saddled with mere suspicions and speculations. 'Eye hath not seen, nor ear heard, neither have entered into the heart of man the things God hath prepared for him.' Our most inventive genius could never have concocted a means for our salvation. After all, we wouldn't even know what to call Him—much less how to be saved—were it not for His revelations."

"We deal with value concepts every day. We may buy goods or services, collect some rare thing, or invest in some market promise, but we sometimes neglect what is our most valuable possession—our soul."

"The providence of God is a fact affirmed in Scripture. However, we are not told how He acts, when, and why. We only know that He does."

Humility

Humility always precedes greatness. The reason?

- ▶ **God cannot use men who are self-employed.**
  Matt 16:24—"If any man will come after me, let him deny himself and take up his cross and follow me."

- **No man can grow until he first sees his own needs.** James 4:6—"Therefore he saith, God resisteth the proud, but giveth grace to the humble."

- **Neither creation or mankind profits from pomposity.** 1 Peter 5:5—"Likewise, ye younger, submit yourselves unto the elder. Yea, all of you be subject to one another, and be clothed with humility: for God resisteth the proud, but giveth grace unto the humble."

- **Besides, great men do not set out to be great.** Luke 9:46–48—"Whosoever shall receive this child in my name receiveth me: and whosoever shall receive me receiveth him that sent me: for he that is least among you all, the same shall be great."

- **Furthermore, truly great men seldom know it.** Proverbs 3:7—"Be not wise in thine own eyes, but fear the Lord."

—That's Life, p. 54

Small Bits

Wisdom is seldom more evident than it is in the man who knows when to be quiet.

Never is talent more enjoyed than when seen in the person who doesn't know he's got it.

Never is a teacher wiser than when he comes to realize that he has at his disposal the opportunity to work great good or great harm.

It's hard to watch where you're going when you don't know where you're going.

Honesty is just as important in the small matters of life as in the bigger ones. Habitual honesty is a conspicuous part of the Christian character. Character is never more clearly illustrated than when the smallest choices in life—choices that seemingly don't even matter much—are made with sincere integrity. A good Christian will develop a determination to practice honesty even when nobody's looking—just because it's right to do so. Actually, to do less is to displace the feelings of special satisfaction that come from right choices in small matters.

To get going means to get up and get at it; but you need to be sure the "it" is worth your getting.

I once visited a little country café (not a restaurant, mind you, but a kaf´-fay). The coffee was hot and black, the pancakes light and fluffy. The waitress—who called everybody "sweetie"—was efficient and kind in her own simple country way. It was just a fine country morning. But it was not the coffee, the pancakes, or the waitress that impressed me the most. What really caught my eye was a picture on the wall—slightly off center—and obviously old. It showed a little baby—bright-eyed, two-teethed, with disheveled hair and a little left-over food on his cute, smiling face. Underneath the picture was a scribbled notation. It said, "I know I'm important, 'cause God don't make no junk!" Small truth, Great lesson.

Permitted Plagiarism

Learn to cope: Everyone has problems—each his own.

1. **Take a deep breath.** Lots of problems will work themselves out, given enough time. Let it wait a day or two, if you can.

A Lifetime of Distilled Wisdom

2. **Don't look too far out.** Nobody knows the future. If you begin to anticipate all the bad things that can happen, you may end up helping them to happen.

3. **Don't be afraid to be honest.** When it comes time, say what you feel—honestly. If it hurt, say so. If you were disappointed, let it be known; but be kind.
   —*That's Life, Too*, p. 76

And could I give you one more bit of *Life By The Numbers?* Here are some simple tips to help with good Bible study:

1. **Find a quiet place.** Interruptions are the most frequent retardants to good Bible study.

2. **Give it all you've got.** You don't have the right to give God second rate concentration any more than to give Him second rate dedication.

3. **Try harder this time.** Study is work. And just because you didn't get it all last time you tried is no reason to quit.

4. **Pray about it.** God will help you if you'll ask Him.

5. **Take your time.** Learning is slow. So is growth. Both take time. But time spent studying God's Word is always worth your while.
   —*That's Life, Too*, p. 76

Short Stuff
God expects that you do your best to reach your spiritual potential. Even if it's hard.

A settlement with mediocrity is the worst of all treaties.

Walter Winchell once said, "money sometimes makes fools of important persons, but it may also make important persons of fools."

Balance is important, no matter what. When something's out of balance, it's hard keep it on track.

A Short Sermon
I sometimes wonder how people get along who have no close connection to God. Notice, I mean by *close* an *intimate* connection. Seems to me there's likely a huge vacuity in the heart that is not in regular contact with Him. How sad not to have Him around every day.

It's true, nearly everybody believes in God—at least at sometime or the other. Maybe at a funeral, or on Christmas morning or at Easter time. But not very many folks have an intimate, every-day connection with God.

To do so you have to have a consistent prayer life. How could that be otherwise? And that connection also implies a familiarity with His Word. How could there be a connection when you don't even know the number to call?

There's more to serving God than merely acknowledging Him. If you pray to God only when you're in trouble, you'd do well to sit down and examine your connection with Him. If you don't have a regular association with His Word, you'd do well to sit down and examine your priorities. If you don't have any contact with Him here, how do you expect to have contact with Him there? I'll tell you one thing: you can't go to heaven if you give God second, or third, or fourth place in your life.

Some Small Thoughts About Words

Words can be builders or they can destroy. A word wisely used is a thing of beauty. A word out of place is absolutely ugly. It takes a good heart and a wise mind to make sure words edify and bring encouragement.

Solomon has considerable to say about the use of words—both wise and unwise. "Death and life are in the power of the tongue" (Proverbs 18:21). Death is separation; life is union. The tongue can bring about fellowship, or it can separate (16:28).

Innuendo is one of the most damaging misuse of words. You don't have to say much to plant a negative thought in the mind of the hearer. Innuendo, properly placed, is little more than a lie. "The words of a talebearer are as wounds and they go down into the innermost parts of the belly" (26:22). The simplest little words can create a train of thought that can run amuck.

And another little thing: a word can have an effect because of who said it. Personality makes words go in different directions sometimes. Being cognizant of your personality—how you are viewed by others—is often a wise way to decide what you say and how you say it.

I have a little note on my desk that has been there for over 25 years. I can see it from where I sit, but the person across the desk can't. It says "Think! God help me to say no more than need be said, and help me to say it softly." That little note has served me well over the years.

Proverbs 13:3—"He that keepeth his mouth keepeth his life; but he that openeth wide his lips shall have destruction." That about says it all.

Some Little Things We All Can Do

One of the best ways to help depression is to get out and do something for somebody. Even if you're not depressed, why not do something for somebody today?

True benevolence is providing for a need without the expectation of anything in return. To expect accolades for extending benevolence is like paying for somebody to notice you.

Pleasure is greatly enhanced by the knowledge that you did it right. One of the great joys in life is a job well done.

Listen to this: it's musical. "Use what you possess; the woods would be very silent if no birds sang except those that sang best" (Henry Van Dyke). Sing. Even if you don't sing well.

If I don't do it because someone else can do it better I never will do it any better.

Letters: What Would I Write?

I was just thinking—

> If I were authorized to write one letter to Jesus, what would I write?

> If I could tell the world what it needs to hear in one paragraph, what would I write?

> If I could address all parents with one piece of advice, what would I write?

> If I could write a verse about my mate, what would I write?

> If I had to describe my life in one paragraph, what would I write?

Leftovers

To be a peculiar person (1 Peter 2:9), you have to be particular—about who and what you are.

Few things are more beautiful than a word well said.

To try and fail is sad, how much more not to have tried at all.

Indifference may well be the bane of our society.

I like what Lawrence W. Bush said: "I think we have one foot in heaven and the other on the banana peel of self-interest."

Just watching the clock never got anybody anything. It's a waste of time.

Short Stuff

A life that is devoid of a careful relationship with God is merely playing at life. To not include Him means that life is little more than a playground.

To inspire others is to inspire oneself.

The greatest friend of Truth is Time, her greatest enemy is Prejudice and her constant companion is Humility.
—*Charles Caleb Colton*

A wise man will ever draw a connection between duty and satisfaction.

Listen a Little
Decline—
- a drop in intensity
- a marked loss of strength or effectiveness
- a slide to a lower level
- a slow deterioration
- a gradual loss of power
- a slow weakening.

I think you get the idea: it's just going the wrong way.

Truth—

It is truth that builds character

It is truth that dispels ignorance, erases superstition, identifies sin.

It is truth that generates faith, that inspires hope, that promotes love.

It is truth that dispels fear, respects honor, encourages courage.

It is truth that demands kindness, recommends piety, promotes obedience.

It is truth that calls for a decision.

Truth reigns! Truth is all about God, God is all about truth.

The Rope of Hope
Hope is called "the anchor for the soul." It is a mental apparatus, based on faith, which reaches off into the future and attaches itself to that which we desire and have a warm expectation of receiving.

A Lifetime of Distilled Wisdom

It's like a rope attached to an anchor and tossed from here to the very throne of God.

When you're down and out and no one seems to care,
pull on the rope.

When you've momentarily lost your way and everything seems blurred,
pull on the rope.

When depression seems your lot and you call out and no one answers,
pull on the rope.

When your friend turns and walks no longer with you,
pull on the rope.

When there is bad new on top of bad news,
pull on the rope.

When you're tired and it still must be done and you feel like you can't go on,
pull on the rope.

When time has eroded your health and this time its worse than ever,
pull on the rope.

When you suddenly realize it's your fault and "I'm sorry" sticks in your throat,
pull on the rope.

When shame and disgrace have cast you into a pit of despair and no one seems to care,
pull on the rope.

When death has come and robbed you of someone near and dear,
pull on the rope.

When you must finally come to face your own mortality,
pull on the rope.

Short Stops

I'd like to say a word about our young Christians around the country. I realize that there are some problems among the young people among us, but I have to tell you: there are some great kids around, too, some great Christian youngsters.

I see them worshiping, faithful in their attendance, always ready to do what they can. I see them acting in a most appropriate manner at the services, as well as out in the world. I see many of them dressed nicely and with modesty. I am impressed with the influence they wield. In fact, if you notice, many of our conversions today are because of some young guy or girl got them interested in the gospel. Look about you on Sunday at how many of our guests were brought by some young person.

And so, in our haste to warn, in our haste to talk to them about "how it was when I was a kid," let's not forget to thank the ones who are outstanding Christians.

Just a Couple of Things

A teacher—of any kind—has at his disposal the opportunity to work great good or inflict great harm.

"Influence" and "influenza" come from the same root. And both of them spread something.

My Heroes

I have lots of heroes. Some of them are friends with whom I have shared precious moments—some good and some not so good—friends like Ed Harrell, Paul Earnhart, Sewell Hall and Brent Lewis, with whom I have laughed, and cried, and prayed and prayed. Russ Bowman is one of my heroes, so is Harold Turner. These are all men of high character, men of great skill, men of devotion to the cause. And there are others—several others.

Some of my heroes are the young preachers with whom I have worked at my home congregation. These are all men of skill and determination. Heroes.

Lots of my heroes are folks nobody ever heard of. Men who pour concrete or fix air conditioners, or do plain office work during the week and preach the gospel at some little-known congregation somewhere on Sunday, men who are so in love with the Lord they can't help but go and do what they can—and at considerable inconvenience. And I deplore that they are called "part-time preachers." They're gospel preachers, folks! Heroes, all.

Some of my heroes are women. Women who quietly go about being a great value to their husbands, who are great examples to their children, who are an unashamed influence at the PTA or the Red Hat Club. Women who are Christians everywhere—at the grocery store, at the soccer field or little league park.

Some of my heroes are the young women who are looking to grow up in the gospel, who want to marry a good Christian rather than a rock star, young women who might even want to—perish the thought—marry a preacher, and spend their years trying to help people go to heaven. My heroes are godly young women who know how to dress; women who know to speak, who know how to listen, how to take a stand without being unkind, how to make a man to become all he was meant to be.

And, as you have likely already noted, some of my heroes are kids—teenagers who are not afraid to confess before their peers their faith in Jesus Christ, some of the older young people who go off to college and unashamedly launch a path of righteousness and probity. My heroes are those little kids who know how to respect the older folks, and have tender hearts, ready to hear and learn. My heroes are those youngsters who can regard talent in others without being jealous, kids who are not the least bit interested in some experiment with the devices of the devil, kids who say what is right and mean it—even if it means they won't be accepted—kids who are not afraid to hug their parents—in public. They don't know how important they are, these young people. My heroes, they are.

My heroes. I wish you knew them all.

Snippets

The devil must have been the one that concocted the idea that looking good is better than being good.

"A man of character finds a special attractiveness in difficulty, since it is only by coming to grips with difficulty that he can realize his potentialities."

—*Charles de Gaulle*

Short Stops

Speaking of potential, are you aware that our word *potential* came from the Latin word for *power (potentia)*? Actually, the root originally meant "to be able." Confer "potent," too.

When it comes to running the Christian's race you have to run it by yourself, and you have to run it all the way out. To quit is to invite not just failure, but disaster.

Man: "seeing is believing." God: "believing is seeing."

One of the most serious cultural contradictions of this age: we are more concerned about the here and now than the hereafter.

Hope

The Hebrew writer says that hope is the anchor for the soul. Having no hope is like a ship's captain with no compass, a runner with no finish line, a mountain climber who has reached the end of his rope. Without hope, there's nothing left.

Hope is a combination of desire and expectation. It is based on the exceeding great and precious promises of God—promises which are sure, about which there is no doubt. Hope is that which reaches off into the future and attaches itself to that which we desire, and which we expect to receive. It's a rope attached to the throne of God. It reaches past the veil. It transcends time and lands in eternity. When we are sad, we have hope. When we are hurting, we have hope. When we are exasperated or disconsolate, there is still hope. Hope never dies for the Christian. When things are bad, he just reaches up and pulls the rope.

Heaven and hope are inseparably connected. Without heaven there is no hope. Without hope, heaven disappears. Hope is what heaven is all about; heaven is what hope is all about. Hope, for the Christian, is the polar star for his soul, the light at the end of the tunnel, the goal that is just around the next bend, that home which is right over the next hill. Heaven and hope are his energy, his motive for keeping on, his reason for peace and quiet in the midst of turbulence and discord.

> **Hope, for the Christian, is the polar star for his soul, the light at the end of the tunnel.**

Blessed be the God and Father of our Lord Jesus Christ, which according to his abundant mercy hath begotten us again unto a lively hope by the resurrection of Jesus Christ from the dead. To an inheritance incorruptible and undefiled, and that fadeth not away, reserved in heaven for you, who are kept by his power, ready to be revealed in the last time (1 Peter 1:3–5).

Be Wise Small

Speak to someone who has a frown on his face.

Ask someone where he goes to services?

Make someone happy by telling them what a good job they do—even if it's small stuff.

Take time to talk with a little kid. After all, "of such is the kingdom…"

"Beware" and "be aware" are akin to each other.

Call somebody way off for whom you care—then tell 'em so.

Read the beatitudes again and see how all these things fit.

Wanna Have A Good Day?

- ▶ Be wise small.
- ▶ Put it back where you got it.
- ▶ Start over and get it right this time.
- ▶ Keep it to yourself.
- ▶ Keep on until you're through.
- ▶ Throw out the trash.
- ▶ Pray.
- ▶ Pray.
- ▶ Pray.

A Lifetime of Distilled Wisdom

Sunday Starters

Practical Pointers From Proverbs (Proverbs 4:5)

Getting a good Sunday start is so important. Here's how.

1. **Get wisdom**—You can't effectively handle life's problems without it.
2. **Get understanding**—If you're going to get there, you have to know the way.
3. **Don't forget what you know**—Re-member it, re-call it, re-collect it or you can't apply it.
4. **Don't turn back**—There's nothing good where you came from, so why turn back?

—*From* The Family Together

Snippets

Foolishness is never more obvious than when the fool who said it doesn't even know it's foolishness.

Bitterness is like sawmill gravy. The more you stir it, the thicker it gets.

It's bad to be sad. It's worse to be glad when you ought to be sad.

"Money and time are the heaviest burdens of life, and the unhappiest of all mortals are those who have more of either of them than they know how to use."

—*Dr. Samuel Johnson*

If the love of money is the root of all kinds of evil, what must the plant look like?

The Little Tree In The Gutter: A Parable

It's just a little twig of a bush. It's in the gutter. The rain gutter of the church building. It's been there since last summer. It's become a favorite of mine.

I watched it all summer long. I figured it would die during the winter; but as I was going to my car this morning, I noticed that it has sprouted some new leaves and is about to start growing again.

It's only about 18 inches tall, and there is not another thing around it. It's all by itself up there in the gutter. I don't know how it got up there. I don't' know where it came from. I just noticed it one day. It was just a little thing then, barely peeking out of the gutter. I started watching it. Almost every day when I'd go to get in the car, I'd just glance up there to see how the little guy was doing. It was doing fine. Nobody saw me do it, but I spoke to it a time or two.

One of the deacons noticed it up there in the gutter and wanted to get up there an chop it down. I protested. Loudly. "Please don't cut that little tree down. It's not bothering anybody. It's just up there doing what it can. I really like that little bushy thing." He left it alone.

That little bush of a thing is not trying to impress anybody with bright leaves or pretty blooms. Its leaves are straggly and its branches thin and crooked. Actually, I guess nobody would look up there and say it's pretty. But you know what? I think it's pretty. It's just being what it is. I like that.

It's not in some fertilized flower bed, not in some fancy pot, adorning some patio somewhere. It's not even out in some field somewhere with a lot of other plants. Never will be. It's just up there in the gutter.

> **It's just being what it is. I like that.**

Nobody tended to it all year. Nobody put fertilizer on in when the spring rains came. It had to grow all by itself up there in the gutter. Nobody trimmed it up this summer. It still looks disheveled, kind of like your hair does when you get up in the morning. Nobody tried to cover it up when we had some unseasonable freezing weather this year. Nobody did anything to help it along. And it still stayed. All by itself—with nobody's help—it stayed.

And something else—I don't know how it keeps from just giving up. Where's it going? What does the future hold for it? Is somebody going to notice it and find a use for it among their floral arrangements? I doubt it. Nobody's likely to even recognize what kind of plant it is, or call it by its botanical name, much less go up there and get it down. But it doesn't get bent out of shape because nobody notices it. The future doesn't look so good I guess. And yet, it just keeps on keeping on.

I love that little tree. I know someday it'll probably blow away, or wash out of the gutter, or just die from old age. I'll feel sad when it happens. That little tree in the gutter may feel like its little life was wasted. But actually, it's helped me. It did what it could with what it had where it was.

I'll hate looking up there one day and seeing just an old empty gutter.

Yes, I Can!

- ▶ I can make today better than yesterday (1 Peter 1:1–2).
- ▶ I can improve what you have that is useful (Galatians 2:2–4).
- ▶ I can diminish the effect of some nagging weakness we drag around (Philippians 3:13–14).
- ▶ I can seek ways to serve others (Galatians 5:13–14).
- ▶ I can live up to my own possibilities (Ephesians 4:15–16).

Forgiveness

There is a lone grave stone in a cemetery not far from New York City. On its rocky face is inscribed one word: *Forgiven*. There is no name, no date of birth, no date of death, no inscription of some passage of Scripture. Only one word: *Forgiven*.

Do you ever long for a few minutes of complete silence during which you can sit and contemplate the fact of your forgiveness?

Are you ever able to sit quietly for a moment—maybe at midday—and define, in your own heart, the meaning of forgiveness.

Have you ever taken long enough to add up all the figures in your life and determine your real worth? And does it not all add up to forgiveness?

Have you ever sat on the front porch and watched the traffic go by and dealt with the sudden realization that nobody seems much concerned about forgiveness?

Have you ever felt the sheer horror, the revolting realization that you are not forgiven?

Have you ever felt at once both the joy and pain of Jesus when he looked down from the cross and said, "Father, forgive them"?

The Ageless Nature Of God's Word

"The intellectual ethic is the message that a medium or other tool transmits into the minds and culture of its users" (Nicholas Carr, *In The Shallows*). In other words, the inventor of the clock had no idea what effect it would have on the world (as today). Before the clock there was only the day—sunrise to sunset. The inventor of the map had no concept of how maps would come to impact society. Look at today's map—it talks back to you—"recalculating!" it says. The inventor of the light bulb had no concept of how that invention would eventually affect the world. Actually, light is everywhere anymore. We have to close the window shades just to get enough darkness to sleep in. The inventor of television, the Internet, the cell phone had no idea the effect these instruments of communication would have on society, or on our minds. They'll all part of our daily lives—actually too much a part, I suspect.

And do you know what's amazing? In the midst of all that changes, no matter the age or the inventions it produces, God's Word remains the same. The reason? People don't change. They have the same problem: Sin. And the answer to their problem remains the same: It's Jesus and His Word.

Snippets

Yesterday is passed. Tomorrow is yet to come. Maybe we should just take care of today.

"When you get to the end of your rope, tie a knot and hang on."
—*Franklin D. Roosevelt*

The best education you'll ever get is to learn as much as you can about who and what you are.

Christianity is a constant course-correcting maneuver.

Nothing is better than the peace that comes from knowing you did your best.

What Work Does
It produces
It exercises
It tires
It satisfies
—*Galatians 6:5–9*

What Truth Is...
It is definitive
It is functional
It is exclusive
—*Psalm 19:6ff*

How To Have A Good Day
Start right.
- With right thinking (Philippians 4:8)
- With care for right things (Colossians 3:1–5)
- With good goals in mind (Matthew 6:33)

Get your guard up early.
- Recognize who is the real enemy (1 Peter 5:8)
- Remember from whence comes your help (1 Corinthians 15:58)

Try to figure the consequences before you act.
- Take heed to where you're headed (1 Corinthians 10:12).
- Remember that sin is a crime against God (Romans 6:23).
- Get an other-worldly view.
- Remember what is the end of all matters (Ecclesiastes 12:13).
- Without God in life, this world has little to recommend it (1 John 2:15).
- Have a good day.

Sometimes I jot down stuff on little pieces of paper, or put them in my journal. For instance:

R. J. Stevens: Who He Really Was

"Being a great singer of songs, being a great teacher of songs, being a great composer of songs, were not the only attributes of R. J. Stevens. He was a Christian, a man of God, a preacher of righteousness, a watchman at the gate of the temple. He was an example of piety and goodness, a practitioner of holiness and sanctity, a man of moral steel. R. J. Stevens was indeed the sweet singer of Israel in our age, but that was only a small part of who and what he was. He was a Christian—a man of God." (A paragraph from the sermon delivered at the funeral of R. J. Stevens, Pasadena, Texas, October 25, 2012.)

For the New Year

I don't even know where I got this, but I found it stuck in some papers. It was faded with age, but alive with truth. I thought I'd share it:

During the new year I will:

- Like Paul, forget those things which are behind and press forward.
- Like David, lift up my eyes to the hills from which my help comes.
- Like Abraham, trust my God implicitly.
- Like Enoch, walk in daily fellowship with my heavenly Father.
- Like Moses, suffer rather than enjoy the pleasures of sin for a time.
- Like Job, be patient and faithful in all circumstances.
- Like Joseph, turn my back on all evil advances.
- Like Gideon, advance even when my friends are few.
- Like Andrew, strive to lead my brother to Christ.

Snippets
"Nothing can be finally explained until God is found."
—*G. Campbell Morgan*

That person who never gives any thought to sin and its consequences is not only foolish, but in great danger.

It's true what Yogi Berra said, "it ain't over til it's over," but it's also true that when it's over, it's over.

A major university in Houston has an annual event, apparently approved by the University, called *Night of Decadence*. And this is quality education?

Indifference may well be one of the truly major enemies of truth.

"It's peculiarly sinuous movements; its silent glide as a form of locomotion, its sinister head, and fascinating look, it vibrant tongue, its peculiar rearing of the head: all contribute to remind man of the peculiar history in which the serpent once shared." (Leopold on Genesis 3:14)

Sometimes I can't even figure out what I can't figure out (in my journal).

It's not *what* you've got, but *who* you've got that counts.

A Challenge
I hope your New Year's resolutions include "be wise small." Not just the resolution, mind you, but the determination to do it. It'll help you.

A challenge: Sit down and write a psalm. It'll take you into the presence of God in a special way. Here's one I did some time ago:

A Psalm

    How worthy art thou, O God,
     How worthy art thou,
    Worthy of praise art thou, O God,
     And worthy of all honor.
    How wonderful is thy name, O God,
     And high it is, and noble,
    How wonderful thy name, O God,
     And worthy of all honor.
    How marvelous are thy works, O God,
     And how they sing thy praise,
    How marvelous are thy works, O God,
     And worthy of all honor.
    How high is thy salvation, O God,
     The power of thy redemption,
    How high is thy salvation, O God,
     And worthy of all honor.
    How beautiful is thy Son, O God,
     The joy of all our hopes,
    How beautiful is thy Son, O God,
     And worthy of all honor.

Facts vs. Fiction

If memory serves, it was Dr. Johnson who said this, in answer to a question by his friend Garrick, an actor.

> A preacher asked an actor, "Why do the discourses of the stage have more effect upon the auditory than those of the pulpit?" "Because," said he, "we treat fiction as though they were facts, and you treat facts as though they were fiction."

Take Time To Be Holy

"Be ye holy, even as I am holy." The words ring as true today as if the ink from the pen of inspiration had not yet dried on the parchment. *"Be ye holy, even as I am holy,"* means being like God; it means there is the need for adopting and maintaining a life of purity and dignity before God and men alike. *"Be ye holy as I am holy"* means that God has made the well-spring for our energy, the motive for our pursuits, the never-changing direction for our hope.

"Be ye holy as I am holy" has to do with the fulfillment of our probation here in a most pure and loving way, with living of our lives according to the manner presented in His Word. It means we spend our lives in a consistent replication of the character of life and devotion to God so brilliantly seen in His Son, Jesus, the Christ.

"Be ye holy, even as I am holy" means seeing the Christ at Nazareth, seeing Him at Capernaum, seeing Him on the mountain of blessing, seeing Him in the wilderness of temptation, seeing Him in the Garden of His passion and on the road to Golgatha, and as He was suspended on the cross. But *"be ye holy even as I am holy"* also means seeing Him as the resurrected One, seeing Him as he returns to His Father, as seeing Him in His Word as He dictates the means and methods for our return to His Father as well, for, said He, "I am the way, the truth and the life; no man cometh to the Father, but by Me."

"Be ye holy, even as I am holy" means being like our Father, a fact for which He so longed that He gave His Son to bring it about.

Look at This

As Christians:

- ▶ We need to know (John 8:32).
- ▶ We need to grow (2 Peter 2:2).
- ▶ We need to show (Matthew 5: 16).

Jesus Was Real

Jesus was a real person. He was born, he grew up, he lived and He died, and He was concerned.

Jesus was a real person. He got tired, frustrated, angry, and He was concerned.

Jesus was a real person. He walked, talked, listened, learned, and He was concerned.

Jesus was a real person. He called, came, went, and came back, and He was concerned.

Jesus was a real person. He agreed. He disagreed. He commended, He reprimanded. And He was concerned.

Jesus died—for you and me.

Jump Starters

Practical Pointers From Proverbs (Proverbs 10:12–17)

Sure ways to make today better:

Verse 12—Keep anger out of reach. Anger agitates. Always.

Verse 13—Try to understand. Ignorance is a harsh taskmaster.

Verse 14—Store up the good stuff. It's the only thing that won't spoil eventually.

Verse 15—Use your funds wisely. Nobody ever said money is not important. Use it well.

Verse 16—Work for right things. Energy spent on wickedness is badly mis-spent.

Snippets
At a conference of sociologists some years ago, "love" was defined as "the cognitive-effective state characterized by intrusive fantasizing concerning reciprocity of amorant feelings by the object of the amorance." Stupid! The Bible says "God is love." How hard is that?

"Show me the men you honor and I will show you what kind of man you are."
—*Thomas Carlyle*

I don't know where I first got this, nor who said it, I just know that I like it. "Don't walk behind, I may not lead. Don't walk in front of me, I may not follow. Just walk beside me and be my friend."

And it was Sir Winston Churchill who said, "We make a living by what we get, we make a life by what we give."

From My Journal
It seems to me that life consists mostly of trying to be the best who-you-are you can be, or coming up to the level of your own potential. That involves basically two things: recognizing your natural bent; and putting into practical reality those things you have, and whatever you can do. But the opportunity and the responsibility are gifts from God. He is consequently involved in all you do, whether you involve Him in it or not. And so, the greatest glory you can give Him, the greatest respect you can pay Him, is to be who you are, and the best who-you-are you can possibly be. Then thank Him for both possibilities.

I Was Just Thinking...
If I could have a private talk with Jesus, what would I talk about? About my job? About my golf game? About my how my boss treats

me? What would I talk about? Or do you think He might talk about heaven—and hell?

If I could have Jesus tell me exactly what I need to hear, what would He say? Would He tell me how I ought to save my money, so as to "get ahead"? Would He tell me how I ought to do to become better known? Would he tell me how to look better or get in better shape? Or might He tell me how to grow up spiritually?

If I could have Jesus tell me where I need to go, what would He say? Would He talk about movies, or ball games, or parties of various sorts? Do you think He might recommend that I attend the services of the saints on the Lord's Day?

If Jesus wrote me a letter what would he say?

Short Stops
When someone begins a letter or an article by telling you how much he loves and appreciates you, you'd better watch out!

"I cannot do everything, but still I can do something: and because I cannot do everything, I will not refuse to do the something that I can do."
—*Edward Everett Hale*

Word Pictures
Our word "subtle" has an interesting history. It was originally a word to describe a knitting process. In fact, the Latin word was *subtilis*, which meant something finely woven. If you had a fine piece of fabric, it might be described as *subtilis*, well-woven. Our word has always had the tenor of "delicate," but it has come to mean, in modern times, "skillful," or "clever," something that is well presented.

Prayer...
Makes us like the Father.
Makes us think about higher things.
Helps us remember who we are.
Helps us remember what He has done for us.
Keeps things lined up like they ought to be.
Keeps us on the right road.
Keeps us in touch with the real reality.
Keeps hope alive and active.

www.warning.com

The inventor of the clock probably had no idea what effect his new toy would have on society. The inventor of the map, likewise, could not have envisioned in his wildest imagination what effect that innovation would have on society. Likewise, the inventor of the telephone, the radio, television, had no notion how far-reaching would be the effect of these new communication "toys" on the coming societies.

Now, what about the Internet, the cell phone, and their attendant columns of quick communication? We have seen immediate effects of these inventions, but we have by no means reached the conclusions they will have. These relatively new innovations will no doubt have huge influences on future generation..

Have a look at what the Internet has to offer. We push a button and there, quick as a wink, is an abundance of information. That process has even added a word to our vocabulary. We call that sort of thing "google-ing." We put a word in and all of a sudden a map appears, complete with the tenths-of-a-mile instructions as to how to get there. And, if you push another button, a three-dimensional picture of our destination appears. All of it in an instant.

Further, the Internet has made possible a joining together of even the most remote parts of the world by what has become an almost world-wide language. English has become the language of the Internet. It regulates everything from air-traffic to business ventures. It dominates the sports world, giving it world-wide usage. English terms are penetrating every language, mostly with terms garnered from the Internet.

The Internet has also fomented a new kind of crime. Internet bandits are making millions of dollars by illegally securing people's credit card numbers or other private investment information. Privacy has been raped by those looking for a fast dollar—or pound—or euro—or franc. Governments are spending millions in order to prevent their most important secret information from being robbed by Internet thieves.

The Internet has also promoted immorality in away that has never before been possible. Pornography is a good example. Pornography, according to recent statistics, produces more income than Major League Football, Major League Baseball, and Major League Basketball combined. And, because it is so private a possibility, no one knows for sure how many homes it has crept into almost undetected. Those who deal with such moral infractions say that pornography is likely the most invasive of all

> **Pornography produces more income than Major League Football, Major League Baseball, and Major League Basketball combined.**

addictions—more difficult to handle than even opium. And the instrument used to stir up these immoral mental journeys is the Internet.

The Internet has produced many good results. And in the contemplation of the bad, let us not forget the good it has done. Education is made accessible to those who heretofore would have had no such possibility. It has put information of all sorts literally at one's fingertips. Every person who has a computer, if he has the

Internet, has the largest libraries in the world in his own home at the touch of a button. The Internet has made ignorance almost impossible—at least blatantly foolish—in this generation.

The Bible believer has all sorts and kinds of study helps at his immediate call. Lessons of various sorts, sermons on almost every subject are available at the touch of a key code. Commentaries, Bible dictionaries, concordances, as well as many translations of the Bible are all over the Internet, and very easy to locate. The interested Bible student has an abundance of information available from Internet sources.

But may I sound another warning? *Facebook, Twitter*, and other social networks, if they are not carefully used, can be dangerous. They can become addictive, robbing their users of valuable time for more important considerations. They can become a virtual gossip-mill. People will say things about other people with impunity on these media it seems. These venues tend to cause people to throw off restraints, and relate information without due consideration as to where it came from, or even if it's true. These media tend to encourage strange and vindictive speech. They can be a "post-office" that is open too long, and make "friends" of the wrong kinds of people. No one that I know of is opposed to keeping in touch with those you love, even enjoying regular visits with those from whom we are separated by time and distance, but it should be done with moderation methinks.

And—and this could be the most important warning I want to make—the Internet addiction has a tendency to fragment our thinking. It makes us think in a hurry, in short spurts, with only scant, sudden, and short-lived bursts of mental energy. Because of the almost instant availability of information, it can cause us to neglect meditation, one of the most valuable of mental processes. And so we make decisions with only shallow thinking and without careful meditation.

If we are not careful we will begin to read in short bursts and with very little consideration to what we are reading. We become so used to the availability of quick information that if it takes more than the length of a twenty-second television commercial to entertain it, we don't have time for it. That's dangerous.

Meditation—the recollection and reconsideration of vital information—is of primary importance to anyone desiring to serve God with all his heart. Meditation takes God's information and with contemplation and spiritual musing, makes it possible for one to worship God in the truest sense of that word, with his whole heart. No hurry. Just to stop and think for a while about who and what He is, about His Son and what He did is one of the great human experiences. To think about forgiveness and what we would be without it, about resurrection and the hope it provides. All it takes is a quiet place and some deliberate, unhurried thought about God—our Father as revealed to us in His Word. Meditation, in the midst of a hurry-up society, is one of life's great pleasures.

"Blessed is the man that walketh not in the counsel of the ungodly, nor standeth in the way of sinners, nor sitteth in the seat of the scornful. But his delight is in the law of the Lord; and in his law doeth he meditate day and night."

Just a little something different, but very important methinks.

Things I Think I Can Do Better

I can pray more often, and more fervently.

I can meditate on God's Word with greater respect and appreciation.

I can care more about my spiritual condition.

I can care more about the spiritual condition of others.

I can invite more Bible conversations.

I can get started—right now.

Snippets

Great quotations from great men are very often great because they call us back to simple truths.

For instance, it was Albert Einstein who said,

> "The important thing is not to stop questioning. Curiosity has its own reason for existing. One cannot help but be in awe when he contemplates the mysteries of eternity, of life, of the marvelous structure of reality."

Yes, and you spell His name G-O-D.

The Christian's armor works only when it is strapped on. It does no good to sit and admire the panoply; you have to make use of it.

Some Short Journal Entries

"It is impossible, I aver, to measure the grace of God. It reaches to the depth of man's sin, and the height of His glory." (April 30, 2009)

"The entire Bible is concerned with who is in control in life. There is never any doubt about that. God is the supreme authority. It is God with whom we have to do. The failure of His creatures to recognize His imperial rule is, and ever has been, the cause of all of men's miseries. Man's failure to admit and submit to the rule of God has brought about sin—man's main malady." (September 13, 2012)

"A path is a way to go. The very concept suggests a moving from one place to another. The just man has a special way to go. His path is like a guiding light, one that illuminates as he goes. As he goes along, the light shines further out in front of him; but only if he keeps going, only if he keeps looking ahead." (December 7, 2006).

"It seems to me that a changed man will tend to change his environment while it is not necessarily so that a change in environment need change the man. In fact, if a man cannot be a Christian where he is, chances are, he could not be one anywhere." (June 4, 1988)

"Life is strange. I was just going along, and suddenly I woke up one morning and I was old." (February 21, 2013)

"Grace describes God's attitude toward man, no matter his condition. No matter how steeped in sin, man is never out of God's sight. No matter how long sin has dominated his life, God is still near and He cares." (June 12, 1999)

"The fulness of that grace is made real in Jesus Christ. There, His grace is personified, illustrated, practicalized. Without Him, no realization of His grace would be possible. Grace and truth are inseparable; there cannot be one without the other. Jesus is the expression of both grace and truth in both His life and His teachings."
"Thanks be to God for His unspeakable grace!" (May 2, 2007)

From My Journal
"Restoration is the obligation of every new generation. To assume that restoration has been accomplished is to lean in the direction of creedal thinking. There is the constant need to re-examine our actions and teachings, and compare them with biblical principles. To merely accept them because that's the way we heard them growing up is dangerous indeed."

To know yourself is the beginning of true knowledge.

Just a Word or Two
The word "candidate" came to us from a Latin word, *candidatus*, which originally meant "one clothed in white." Wonder what happened?

"Wisdom" is the ability to take good information and create a useful application out of it.

The Simplicity of God's Plan:

- ▸ The entry of Jesus was done without highfalutin credentials, no priestly training, no fancy garments. He just went about with a simple people-message.
- ▸ The message itself was simple, to the point. There was no religious verbiage, no sanctimonious terminology—just a message recommending a return to God. "The common people heard him gladly."
- ▸ The miracles of Jesus were done without fanfare, for they needed no fancy introduction, no musical accompaniment, no dulcet-toned announcer to proclaim their source. Love, compassion, revelation were His tools.
- ▸ Twelve men were not an army. But it was enough.
- ▸ When He sent the Apostles out, two-by-two, there was no mention of some big evangelistic program they were to follow, some fancy organization to get it done—just a love for truth and for the souls of men.

Someone Said...

"A Bible that is falling apart often belongs to someone who isn't."
    Someone handed me that. It's good.

"When Jesus comes, the shadows depart."
    Inscription on a Scottish castle.

Reminds me of a line in John Keble's famous hymn:
    "Sun of my soul, thou Savior dear.
    It is not night if thou be near."

Natural vs. Unnatural Disasters

Disasters, catastrophic events of all sorts are written on the pages on of man's history. Earthquakes, volcanic eruptions, tsunamis, tornadoes, hurricanes, floods, droughts dot the reports of our history. Seldom does time pass very long before some disaster disrupts man's tranquility.

In May, A.D. 526, an earthquake struck in Antioch in Syria. The death toll was estimated at 250,000. We gasp in horror at the imagination of such an imposing event.

One of the most cataclysmic and tragic events in all of human history took place when Mt. Vesuvius erupted in A.D. 79 near the Gulf of Naples. The city of Pompeii was literally buried amid ten feet of dust and ashes. Bodies were petrified by the heat and volcanic dust, thousands of people perished in the wake of the volcanic break-out. We are dismayed even today at the thought of such an horrible happening.

And not far away from our present memory is the earthquake/tsunami that recently rocked Japan. Because we live is such an Internet-ready era, we actually witnessed—with amazement and horror—as towns were literally being swept away. Buildings—over 130,000 of them—looked as if they were being dissolved in the force of the turbulent waters. We cried at the sight of those who looked for their relatives in the midst of the morass of debris, we felt sadness as some carried their dead to somewhere other than home. We were forever touched by the event.

But what brings a greater lamentation, what causes a intense feelings of pity and sympathy is when the tragic events are close to home.

Think again of 9-11. We each know where we were when that terrible man-made earthquake toppled one of our landmarks and killed those whom we love. It was a national disaster, one very close to home, and it produced in each of us not only strong feelings of fear for our own safety, but intense, almost empathetic feelings of pain for those we saw crying out at the loss of their loved ones.

Then there's the more recent heart-rending Newtown event—the classroom killings of young children and teachers with seeming disregard for life. Who among us was not horrified—absolutely taken by grief—at the sight of those waiting for news about their little ones? And did we not groan in front of the television as the news came, "it was one of mine"? What feelings of pain and sorrow that murderous event brought upon each of us! It felt so close to home.

The Boston Marathon—marred and scarred forever by the uncaring hand of some idiot who has no regard for life or limb—one who would take so tranquil a thing as a home-cooker and turn it into some deadly bomb intended to disrupt, dishonor, and demean the very mankind to which he is himself connected. Now it will be marked forever as something like the "Boston Marathon Murders," or "The Boston Marathon Massacre" or some other disturbing name . How sad! How we hurt when we saw the little boy's picture—he who was just waiting to hug his mother when she finished the race. And how sorrowful we felt when we heard the news of the injured—many of who lost limbs or suffered shrapnel-induced injuries to various parts of their bodies. We felt with the Bostonians, we mourned with the survivors, we shed tears. It came mighty close to home.

> **We are so forever touched by their losses. And well we should be. They come close to home.**
>
>

And so, we are hurt and dismayed about the events of Antioch and Pompeii. We are dissettled at the thought of some catastrophe such as that which took place in Japan.

But we are even more disturbed by the events closer to home and those closer to our time—9-11, Oklahoma City, Columbine, Colorado. We cry out in disgust and speak words of sorrow in an effort to comfort those who cannot even hear us. We are so forever touched by their losses. And well we should be. They come close to home.

But may I ask something?

But what about those people right in our community who are walking near the edge of an soon-to-erupt moral volcano, and who don't even see it coming?.

What about the literally hundreds of people who are in the realm of our influence who need to be warned about the coming of a terrible moral tsunami which is presently zooming toward them with a devil's intensity?

What about the young people who are tottering on the brink of a pit of moral decadence, or being immersed in a wave of immorality. Are they not close to home? And should we not say something to them?

What about the thousands of people who are dying each day without Christ, who have no hope of heaven—people whom we might help? Where is our sympathy for them, where are our cries, our lamentations for lost people? Do we walk by unconcerned? Hurricanes are coming! There's a tornado watch! Do we not need to warn them? Are we not to be the world's watchmen? Are we not charged to warn others about the pitfalls of sin? Are we going to walk by, holding the truth in our hand, and offer nothing to those who need it?

Take a Few Minutes Today and...

- Realize full well from whence this day is come (Psalm 118:24).
- Get in touch with your own spirituality (Acts 17:26–28; Colossians 3:1–2).
- Put a guard on your mouth (Proverbs 4:24).
- Do what you do well (Ecclesiastes 9:10).
- Scour off the bad stuff (Ephesians 5:27).
- Be wise small (Proverbs 24:3).

Snippets

"Try hard!" it seems to me, is redundant. There's no other way.

Every one writes his own book of life. Some chapters have lots of question marks, some lots of commas, but all have a new page every day. It's how we use it that matters.

God notices small acts of kindness as surely as large acts of benevolence, so it behooves us to be wise small.

To refuse to listen to God's Word is like a man dying of cancer refusing to hear the remedy for his disease. Only worse.

Be Wise Small Suggestions

"A word fitly spoken is like apples of gold in pictures of silver." Some smallish suggestions for words fitly spoken for today:

- Give someone a word of encouragement (Proverbs 10:20–21; 17:17).

- Speak to someone who needs it a word of kindness (Proverbs 15:4).
- Correct some erring one, but carefully (Proverbs 12:17–18).
- Encourage someone to greater confidence in Christ (Proverbs 3:25–26).
- Talk to your own self about the dangers of a wrong course (Proverbs 4:14–15)

There are many and varied attitudes toward truth. *Be wise small* and see where you fit.

- The "I don't care attitude" (Romans 1:18–24).
- The "I care but won't do" attitude (Acts 26:28).
- The "I do, but don't know" attitude (Romans 10:1–3).
- The "I do, because I know" attitude (James 1:21–25).

Things that militate against humility: (*Be wise small*, or they'll sneak up on you!)

- There is a strong tendency in our society toward personal "rights" without any regard for being "right" according to His Word. (Psalm 119:105)
- There is a continual recommendation of subjectivism. (Matthew 16:24)
- There is a constant approval of self-aggrandizement. (Matthew 23:5–11)
- True humility begins by taking three steps down. (Matthew 5:3–5)

That Peer Pressure
Submit to pressures from peers
   and you move down to their level.
Speak up for your own beliefs and
   Invite them up to your level.
If you move with the crowd, you'll
   get no further than the crowd.
When 40 million people believe in
   a dumb idea, it is still a dumb idea.
Simply swimming with the tide
   gets you nowhere.
So, if you believe in something that is good,
   honest, and bright—stand up for it.
Maybe your peers will get smart and drift your way.
—The Wall Street Journal

Even the media gets it right sometimes.

Word of the Month Club
We are all faced with various decisions that must be made. Every day they come. One of the best ways to take care of decisions—even the little ones—is to deliberate carefully the choices and their possible results.

Our word **deliberate** is from a Latin verb *deliberare,* which is derived from the word *librare,* which originally meant "to weigh." And *lirare* is from *libra,* which originally meant "a balance," or "a pair of scales." It behooves us to **deliberate** carefully and make our choices using the scales of God's Word so as to make sure we have a right standard of measurement, be the choice large or small.

Books Worth a Read
There are several new works written by our brethren which are worthy of a read—among them:

Glimpses Of Eternity—Paul Earnhart

Correction Vs. Mercy—Gardner Hall

Enthusiastic Ideas—Gary Henry

The Big Picture—Marc Hinds

One Another Christianity—Roger Hillis

Understanding Apocalyptic Literature—Mark Roberts

Read a good book lately?

Snippets
You can't really be who you're not, so there's no sense in trying. You can become the best who you are you can be, so there's every reason for trying.

When even a beautiful house is left alone, it tends to rot. 'Tis the same with the soul.

Misused and misguided love is repulsive!

"He that believeth and is baptized shall be saved"? Can than mean something other than what it says?

Try to do what your ability will not allow and you will eventually end up doing nothing.

Paragraphical Ponderings

Preachers should never have to preach on attendance. It should be obvious that when a Christian does not care to attend all the services, his interest is elsewhere. It is foolish to assert that we need a passage which pronounces *anathema* on those who don't come on Sunday and Wednesday night. We don't need one. All we need show is that interest and attendance are connected and that a person who is truly interested will attend.

Now you try to explain that away all you want and when you are finished, it will still say the same thing: a person who is able yet, does not attend the services is not interested in what is going on at the services. Bring your excuses, pronounce your justifications, and rationalize all you want. And when you are done, the parable of the sower will still affirm the same thing: prepared soil is the only kind which results in good fruit.

Spiritual maturity is what the Bible is all about. Oh sure, it tells you how to be born into God's family; but the rest of the space is intended, in various ways, to help you mature in the faith, to make you strong and vibrant in your determination, to ascertain spiritual ways to sustain your journey toward home, regardless of external influences.

Without spiritual maturity, the soul flounders and vacillates, and is driven by various winds of doubt and speculation. Without that maturity, the soul is subject to evil influences and all manner of sinful temptations.

The soul that is mature, conversely, is able to detect a proper course of action and progress, even in the most difficult of circumstances. Spiritual development is the basis for spiritual progress.

—*From* Just A Minute, *p. 107*

A Lifetime of Distilled Wisdom

Some Things We Can Learn From David's Encounter With Goliath

How to handle criticism. David's brothers were critical of his actions, but that didn't deter him. You will be criticized if you follow Jesus.

The value of self-evaluation. David was not boastful or arrogant, but when the time came to act, he already knew what he could do. To be ready to help, we must first find ourselves, assess our talents and know our limitations. Faithful services depends on knowing ourselves.

Not to be intimidated by the opponent. Surely David took note of the size of the giant. Surely he must have compared his size and abilities with the size and abilities of the Gathian. But that didn't keep him for doing what he could. We, too, will have giants—big obstacles—in our lives, but we must not let that keep us from our service.

To use what you have. The giant was a man of war from his youth. He had all the tools, all the knowledge and experience. But David had God. And he knew that with God and a sling shot and stone, he was bigger than the giant with all his accouterments of warfare. What faith! We need to see from whence comes our strength and help, and realize that when God is on our side, we don't need anything else.

Things You Should Tell Your Children

Parents have lost control in far too many homes today. Oh, they provide, but I'm not at all sure many of them are providing what the children really need, even among believers. When we come to emphasize baseball and soccer to the exclusion of the Lord's work, we have voluntarily surrendered control of our children. When television, the Internet, and social media become the teachers, we are no longer doing the job we agreed to when we brought these little people into the world. Now, nobody is saying that it's wrong for the youngsters to participate in extra-curricular activities. In fact, these activities, properly managed, are good for our children. It's just that, in far too many instances, the emphasis on these things and things like them, tend to dominate not only the children's thinking, but our thinking as well.

Children are sponges. They want to know. They are looking for instruction, for examples of what is right and proper—even in their teenage years. They want to know what is important, what is valuable. It's up to us as parents—even as grandparents—to make sure that what they digest is actually what is vital for their well-being—both physically and spiritually.

I would like to suggest some things you should impress upon the minds of your children. What I want to suggest are spiritual necessities; you're already aware, I am sure, about what are their physical necessities. I believe these things not only to be important, but vital to the spiritual maturing process of every child.

To think about, love God. Children need to be taught early on what God says is the first and most vital commandment, "Thou shalt love the Lord, the God, with all thy heart, with all thy soul, and with all thy mind. And the second is like unto it, Thou shalt love thy neighbor as thyself" (Matthew 22:39–40). If a child is taught to respect and admire these two commandments early on, they will likely be fine guides for life. They should be not only taught, but illustrated in the lives of parents, so that the children actually observe the actual use of these commands by their parents. And not just when they are little, either. And remember, inculcation is the key to learning, so repeat, repeat, repeat.

To be thankful. Our blessings—particularly in this nation and at this point in time—are multitudinous. Children need to know that our blessings come from God, and they need to hear us thank Him for them regularly. When children are taught early on that blessings are gifts from God, they tend to become aware of how fortunate they are instead of taking for granted all that they have. Thanksgiving should be a part of every family prayer. Paul said, in Colossians 3:15, "…and be ye thankful." David, in the 95th Psalm, said, "…let us make a joyful noise to the rock of our salvation, let us come before his presence with thanksgiving." It is God from whom all blessings flow. Young people need to be made aware of that—as babes, but as teenagers as well.

> **Children need to know that our blessings come from God, and they need to hear us thank Him for them regularly.**

That true love is more than mere physical attraction. Children need to be taught early on about true love and what it actually is. As they grow, they need to be taught about the difference in love and lust. The choices they make as they mature will be made better if they have been taught that love is kind, considerate, patient, behaves properly, is not self-seeking, etc. (See 1 Corinthians 13). If that youngster understands true love, his choices will be better, his life easier and more enjoyable. And every child needs to remember to "behold what manner of love the Father hath bestowed upon us, that we should be called the sons of God…" (I John 3:1). What a blessing to understand true love!

To remember his influence. A youngster who has been taught that others are watching is less inclined to make mistakes; and when he does, to correct them early. One who understands that he has influence on others will be careful to let his light shine, so that others, seeing his good works, will more likely be constrained to glorify the Father (see Matthew 5:13–14). Young people need to know how to protect their influence, knowing that it is a part of character development.

To have his own faith. Children need to understand that while they may inherit certain characteristics from their parents, even monetary values, they do not and cannot inherit their faith. Faith comes from hearing the Word of God—for yourself. Nobody can do that for you. (See Romans 10:17.) Furthermore, everyone must rely on his own faith. Faith is critical. By it we please God and serve men. Without it we cannot be and do all that God expects of us. Children need faith-building lessons and faith-building examples at every level of their maturity.

Rearing children is not for the faint of heart, nor is it for the procrastinator. It is a work of the highest import, but one of great joy when it results in faithful children, serving the Lord with all the love and passion they received from godly parents. But one final word of warning: every person is his own person. Some will not be faithful, regardless of the godly instruction. All we can do is the best we can do. Then pray.

Four Ways To Make a Good Day Even Better

- ▶ Look for some way to compliment someone—especially the poor or less fortunate (Galatians 6:10).
- ▶ Find the courage to insert God into the conversation (Proverbs 19:17).
- ▶ Pray an ardent prayer of thanksgiving for your family (Psalm 100:1–4).
- ▶ Look up instead of in or out—all day (Psalm 1:1–2).

I Don't Know Why

I don't know why we try so hard to define what is immodest apparel when everybody knows what it is!

I don't know why it's so hard for us to define what gossip is when everybody knows, for having done some of it.

I don't know why we can't see that too much entertainment robs us of our spiritual energy.

I don't know why we can't be as tolerant of others as we are of ourselves.

Sermon Outline

I'm writing a sermon outline today. May I share with you its major points?

Religion Without God

1. Religion without authority is religion without God.
2. Religion without commitment is religion without God.
3. Religion without moral restraint is religion without God.
4. Religion without judgment is religion without God.

From My Journal

"Was just thinking today—

> The spirit of competition is dangerous. It's only about a half inch from envy.
>
> Nature speaks volumes, but it doesn't tell us all there is to know about God.
>
> Death is hard, no matter how ready you think you are. After all, we've never been on the other side.
>
> Writing is hard. Fact is, I can't say much that's not already been said, probably better than I can say it.
>
> Time, by itself, doesn't really mean anything, but what you do with it means everything."

Be Wise Small Snippets

It is very often the case that decadence follows luxury.

The effective teacher has at his disposal the opportunity to do great good or great harm.

A good attitude is much like a pure motive; one is no good without the other.

Character is never developed without suffering some difficulties or stern corrections of some sort to help shape it.

Wisdom and perspicuity run on the same track. Both are the ability to see the end of the thing from the beginning.

Living life is much like chopping cotton—you have to take it a weed at a time.

Stuff I See

Sometimes, I like to just write about stuff I see. For instance, you ever try to describe a scene featuring the beauty and grandeur of God's nature? Here's an effort—a piece from my journal written several years ago while I was in a meeting in Oklahoma.

I shake myself awake a few minutes before six A.M. A lush symphony has already commenced. The winds on which were borne last night's cool front have subsided and the sun has just now timidly peeked over the small mountain which is visible from the window of my east room. The air is filled with sound—rich, pulsating sound. From the open window it rushes on to wherever sound goes. In the far distance a bird sets the tone with a beautiful whistle which moves up and down in almost perfect harmonic thirds. Somewhat closer, a crow gives out his guttural "caw," as a bobwhite quail introduces itself over and over again as if in some sort of competition, each of his chirps getting higher and higher. The ever-present rooster has not the most beautiful, but perhaps the most distinctive of the warm morning sounds. His cock-a-doodle-do introduces the dawn.

There are so many different pitches, so many tempos, a diverse number of ranges, and a multitude of moods in the morning sounds. Yet each is playing a part. They are all congenial, each fitting perfectly into what almost seems to be a scored melody. Together they seem to form a natural symphony, a fitting tribute to a most lovely early June morning.

I hear the climax to the concert just as the sun breaks fully over the mountain and bathes the small valley with hues of purple and shimmering gold. I get out of bed and pull on my jogging stuff. With an anticipation I don't usually have at home, I tie my shoes and smooth the humps from my tasseled hair. Quickly I am out the door, careful not to awaken anybody. Down the lane I go. I stumble a bit at first, due to the steep gravel path which leads away from the house and down to the main road. The gravel crunches beneath my feet. Up ahead as small rabbit darts out of the brush. He stops, perks up his velvety ears, and upon hearing my step, darts back into his hiding place, his white tail shining brightly in the morning sun. As I turn back east, I can see a slight fog forming in the valley before me. It's just enough to give the scene an almost ethereal glow. I glance back north. I can see a number of layers of depth, as the hills jut out from the small rise in the road and slant down toward the creek. I hear it plainly long before I get to it. The sound of the little creek grows louder with each step, and seems to intensify in perfect time with my now heavy breathing.

Off to the left there is the sweet smell of new mown hay (I had heard the tractor yesterday) and to my right trees are bearing all manner of vines, almost like an animal might caress her young. There is still the last vestige of the morning concert, too; but now the birds are out, darting to and fro in what seems an effort to

BE WISE SMALL

catch the sun's rays which have now begun to punctuate the early morning haze.

I am now at the creek. Its sounds are happy, even somewhat playful as it tumbles over the rocks, gleefully reflecting the sun's rays which by now are filtering through the trees.

The sound of the old rickety bridge thunders under my feet as I cross, each echo almost stepping on the one just before it.

As I turn south now, the trees have formed a canopy over the small road, and the temperature has dropped sharply in the resulting shade. It seems that the road, with its overhanging trees and clinging vines, has been formed into a conduit for my route back home.

> **I am now at the creek. Its sounds are happy, even somewhat playful as it tumbles over the rocks.**

Up on the hill I see an unpainted house, next to it a well with a rusty chain clamped to on old galvanized bucket. The little pasture in front of the old place forms a scene right off a Windberg painting, And could I paint it as I saw it, he would offer me no competition.

By now I've gotten my "second wind" and turned back toward the house. It's the same path, but my view of it has changed. It's every bit as beautiful going back as it was coming. The shadows are now in front of me, the menagerie of sights and sounds has now become enhanced by the light which dances almost hypnotically from tree limb to tree limb. I see a dead snake, hit by a passing car no doubt, and I'm sorry he had to die outside the realm of nature, even as much as I dislike snakes.

I cross over the bridge, breathing heavily now, grab a deep breath, and start back up the slow gravel incline. Before me is a demonstration of the handiwork of God—green lush, rich with sound, and permeated with a sweet morning aroma that only God could give it.

Off to the left in the ditch I see a beer can, indisputable proof of man's inordinate fondling of God's nature. I turn toward the Davises, my home for the week, just glad to be a part of it all.

And that's my morning symphony. But would you want to hear it all better said? Here 'tis:

> The heavens declare the glory of God; and the firmament showeth His handy-work. Day unto day uttereth speech, and night unto night showeth knowledge. There is no speech nor language, where their voice is not heard.

Personality Considerations For Private Moments

    Consider the faith of Abraham

    Consider the moral strength of Joseph

    Consider the sensitive heart of David

    Consider the wisdom of Solomon

    Consider the love of Ruth

    Consider the trials of Jeremiah

    Consider the folly of Gehazi

    Consider the endurance of Job

    Consider the love, respect, devotion of the Apostles of Jesus

    Consider the foolishness of Ananias and Sapphira

    Consider the courage of Stephen

    Consider the perseverance of Paul

    Consider the death, burial, and resurrection of Jesus Christ

I Was Just Thinking...

It's not yesterday or tomorrow, but today we need to be thinking about.

Some people seem to think Charles Herguth was right when he said, "truce is better than friction."

Anger, long tolerated, can fester into a large sore.

Just because you struck out doesn't mean you're out of the game.

Imitation is foolish. You can't be who you're not, no matter how hard you try.

Our lack of talent or our inadequacies should not cause us to lie to others about who and what we are.

Adversity is part of living life. It comes to us all. It's about how we handle it that counts. I believe it was Bertha Callaway who said, "We cannot direct the winds, but we can adjust the sails." How true!

"How old is the baby? I asked. "Six weeks," she replied. "You've known that child for only six weeks," I said, "and you would stand in the front of a Mack Truck to keep it from hitting it." Little ones teach us a lot about love, don't they?

I used to think that the great men in life were the strong. Now, I think the best men in life are the humble—they're the strongest of all.

Tears are not always bad. They sometimes wash away the bad stuff.

Leftovers

Here are some leftovers from my *That's Life* book of several years ago:

Would someone please explain to me:

- ▶ How we can get so upset over people who kill whales and show no remorse at all for the thousands of babies killed each month by abortions?
- ▶ How we can give movies a rating and leave television alone? I mean, the evening news is everything else but PG-13.
- ▶ How can we always see each others' faults, foibles, and personality quirks, but are blind to our own?
- ▶ How can we teach our children the necessity of honesty and then allow them to hear us say, "Tell 'em I'm not here" when we don't want to talk on the phone; or call in sick when the World Series is on; or make flimsy excuses why we don't want to attend Bible study.

Behold the goad: Lots of people nowadays are more interested in profits than prophets.

One of the most repugnant scenes in life is watching a person smoking a cigarette while standing the line to pay for groceries with food stamps.

I have a strong feeling that ingratitude may be the besetting sin of our society.

Lots of people are attached. Few are involved.

To seek after a quality life without involving God in it is like trying to play football, well, without the football.

We're all just parts, nobody's the whole.

"God is good" is redundant. God is.

People who constantly criticize are very often facing the wrong direction.

Short Stops

"Someday" has ruined many a worthwhile project.

Disappointment sometimes makes happiness happier when it returns.

Knowledge has little value until it is honed into wisdom.

Silence is a gift we don't often utilize.

Conversation is much better when more than one person is involved in it.

If you want someone to stop listening, just start bragging about yourself.

Humility is a funny thing; the minute you say you got it, you lost it.

I-ddiction

I don't know whether or not Al Gore invented the Internet. I only know that it has had the most profound influence of any innovation since Gutenberg invented moveable type for the printing press. Like most other inventions, that influence is both good and bad. The modern-day computer, dressed up in its finest Internet garments, has made its way into business, medicine, politics, as well as other lesser areas of life. It has been good for most of these fields of endeavor, but it has brought decay and deterioration to some areas.

The Internet has come to dominate us. We are in the clutches of *I-ddiction*. We are *I-ddicted*.

One of its most pervasive entries has been in the field of entertainment where, in my opinion, it has done more harm than good. We have become immersed in a sea of entertainment in this generation. We have to have it. Every day. Its influence is everywhere—it's seen in how we walk and talk, how we dress, how we say what we say, and a host of other things. Even many religious leaders today are little more than entertainers. Almost everything we do is influenced by who and what is popular.

Perhaps the most significant and onerous contribution *I-ddiction* has brought to today's world is it's unabashed provision of pornography. Pornographic participation as easy as tapping a tab. What was once available only with considerable effort is not just easily obtained, but because moral restraints are so relaxed, almost-pornographic scenes appear virtually everywhere in some form or the other—in the movies, in some commercials, even occasionally on news programs. It's almost as if today's media is accepting the use of pornographic scenes; there are but a few restraints. Those who have studied pornography's influence say it is a multi-billion dollar business.

The social media craze is another sign of today's *I-ddiction*. Its influence is astounding. And it's not only addicted people of the world—those who have little or no spiritual inclinations—but it has captured the imagination of numerous Christians, who almost without realizing it, have become *I-addicted*. I've been home with people after a preaching service when they hardly entered the house before they grabbed the iPad, Kindle or iPhone to face the day and twitter some time talking about stuff which has little or at least relatively little benefit. It almost insults the guest when someone can't go to the refrigerator without taking the instrument of their satisfaction with them. And the conversation? There are only fragmented sentences, calculated to recognize your presence, not converse with you. After all, we've got to look at the real screen of life, don't you know?

I recently passed two ladies in a grocery store, both of whom were talking on their iPhones. They were somewhat offended when I asked if they were talking with each another.

I-ddiction is dangerous, both in potentiality and reality. It can gradually erode away spirituality by robbing one of time for prayer, meditation, or private worship. Or, it can openly and unabashedly take you places you shouldn't go by offering a satisfaction once reserved only for those who could find the street with the red lights. Furthermore, the social media addict tends to suffer a breakdown of his restraints. People will put pictures on *Facebook* they would not even post on the mirror in the bedroom. The *I-ddict* will say things on the social media pages he would not dare say in a face-to face conversation. Gossip proliferates at a staggering rate in the social media. Innuendo and half-truths are told with impunity and without any feelings of conscience. And what's sad is that most of the people using the social media don't even know what it's doing to them.

And what about *I-ddiction* and the family? Fathers, in far too many homes, take a back seat to the instructions given to their family on *Facebook* or *Twitter*. In too many homes, both the parents and the kids are *I-ddicts*. Mothers are often so busy with their social media friends that they have little time to be keepers at home, much less develop caring and loving relationships with the children. Grandparents who may have little to do with the Internet don't even have enough acceptable parlance to carry on an intelligent conversation with their grandchildren. And sadly, even some of them have become *I-addicted* because it's about the only way they can have a relationship with the grandchildren.

I worry about what *I-ddiction* is going to do to us. Remember the story about the Tower of Babel in Genesis 11? When God saw that man's pride had totally consumed him, do you remember what He decided to do about it? He confounded their language. We are, in my most humble estimation, headed headlong into a re-play of the attitudes that caused the proposal for the Tower of Babel. English is the language of the word in this *I-generation*. It won't be long, methinks, until everyone will be even more highly influenced by what is on the Internet. And don't you think the devil knows that? And don't you think he'll use that?

But there's another side to the story we're telling. The Internet is not inherently evil, nor are the social media outlets it has spawned. The Internet and its social media companions provide probably the most potentially effective medium for the propagation of the gospel ever before known. Almost everybody almost everywhere has an iPad, Kindle or cell phone. That means the social media can take the gospel anywhere we want it to go any time we choose. And at little if any cost. Sure, it takes a little nerve, but just because it does is no excuse for not making God's gospel available for any who will hear it anywhere in the world. And it doesn't have to be some formal web page, either. It can be a simple Facebook-to-Facebook conversation by two people who are looking for God. In fact, that may well be at once the most effective and yet the most neglected way of getting out the message of salvation to a lost world. It's how it was done in the New Testament—they just went everywhere preaching the Word—person-to-person. Will people hear? Not many. But how do we measure the value of one soul? Mostly, it's just a matter of facing the facts and putting the information out there for the "whosoever will may come."

By the way, do you know anyone who is an *I-ddict*?

Snippets

I sometimes wish I had done what I could with what I had when I could. It makes me think of James 4:17.

What I call "put-off-ism" has done great damage to spirituality. It makes me think of James 2:27.

Many a good project has failed out of what I call "afraid-ism." It makes me think of Philippians 4:13.

Another dangerous *ism* is "critic-ism." It makes me think of Proverbs 10:11.

Worship
Do you know what worship does for you?

- ▶ Worship makes you stronger (Hebrews 10:23–25)
- ▶ Worship strengthens your hope (Psalm 95:6)
- ▶ Worship inclines your heart to spirituality (John 4:23)
- ▶ Worship keeps you in touch with eternity (John 9:31)

Take Time To Love
I heard my wife reading the Bible—out loud. It warmed my heart. I thought about how much she has meant to me. I sat down and wrote this:

Do you have a wife who takes care of you, keeps you in her love, makes your house into a home? Who is never too busy to listen when you're disturbed, who is always ready with a word of encouragement, who loves you enough to tell you when you're wrong, but doesn't mark you off when you fail? Who tolerates your unshaven face and dirty blue jeans, who thinks you're handsome, even when you're not? Do you have wife that loves you? Stop and thank God for her, but don't forget to thank her, too. Be sure you take time to love your wife.

Do you have a husband who is the head of your house, who works hard to have a godly faithful family, who has time to listen when you're sad and rejoices with you when you're glad. Who thinks you're cute even with your hair in rollers and your make-up smeared, who is your one and only, who loves God and loves you? Stop and thank God for him. And don't forget to thank him, too. Be sure you take time to love your husband.

Do you have kids in your family that are willing to put down the iPhone or iPad and turn off the TV long enough to listen to what you're saying, who are respectful even when they don't understand, who react to your instructions and corrections with respect, and regard your advice as worth listening to, who don't get upset when you stop everything to read the Bible, or discuss Sunday's sermon in the middle of dinner, who respect your love for their mother, and who notice that you treat her lovingly, who like to hear you pray and who want to be like you? If so, why don't you stop for a minute and thank God for your kids. And don't forget—it might be good to just tell them so. Be sure you take time to love your kids.

> **Be sure to take time to love...**

Do you a friend who has stuck with you through thick and thin, through highs and lows, who has tolerated your strange notions and strange ideas, who has actually kept quiet when you told him or her things you didn't want known, who has been there when there were problems in the family, or when death had robbed you of someone special? Who stood by you when you lost the job or who actually rejoiced at your promotion when they didn't get one? Do you have trouble being nice when your friend is not particularly nice to you? And are you afraid to say how much you appreciate someone whom you appreciate? Are you blessed with a good friend?

Then tell them so! Say it! Are you afraid to say "I love you"? Do the words stick in your throat? God was not ashamed to say "I love you," even when we didn't deserve it, why should you be? Be sure to take time to love your friends.

Do you ever think about how hard it must be for those who are charged with the responsibility of tending the flock of God? You ever think about how hard it must be for them to chide someone who misses services to do some menial thing or participate in their favorite hobby in preference to meeting with the saints? When you pray, do you ever take them into your prayers, do you really appreciate the fact that they watch for your soul, care about your spiritual welfare, try to encourage your faithfulness, try to promote your spiritual growth, that they care enough to correct your path when it's obvious you're headed in the wrong direction? Do you ever think about how hard it must be for them to tolerate your disagreement with some plan or your failure to participate because you didn't particularly like it? Do you appreciate them? Do you love them? Then why not tell them so? Be sure to take time to love those who lead you.

And what about Jesus? Do you love Him? Do you ever just stop what you're doing and think about how much He loved you, how much He sacrificed to make you know that? Do you respect Him? Do you take time to listen to Him? Do you regard highly His commands and respect His ways in all that you do? And when He requires something that you don't particularly want to do, do you turn away—or make excuses? Do you just not pay attention, or do you put it off until another day? If you don't obey Him, you lose Him. Do you believe that? Jesus loved you enough to die for you. Why not stop for a few minutes, get off the roller coaster of life and just tell Jesus how much you love Him? Be sure you take time to love the Savior and Lord.

Best Be Careful!

When a person delights in finding something wrong with others, something's wrong.

When a person can't tolerate in others that which they tolerate in themselves, something's wrong.

When a person rejoices at another person's mistakes, he makes a mistake.

When a person sees in others what he can't seem to see in himself, he's not looking good.

When a person holds a grudge, he holds on to nothing.

When a person can't see another person's talent because he's so focused on his own, his vision is poor.

When a person is so supercilious that you can't even get close to him, he's silly.

Sunday Morning Starters
Proverbs 8:6–10

Get acquainted with a lady called *Wisdom* before you leave for services this morning. She will do you well.

  Verse 6—She will tell you of excellent things, things that have real value.

  Verse 7—She will tell you the truth—even if it hurts a little.

  Verse 8—She will steer you in a righteous way; you can trust her.

  Verse 9—She will help you understand; that way you won't be easily fooled.

  Verse 10—She is more precious than silver or gold; how can you beat that?

Be Wise Small Bits

I sometimes think I was better off when I didn't know everything about everything that's going on everywhere.

Raising kids is kind of like flying a kite—pull the string too tightly and the string breaks and the kite flies away, leave it too loose and the kite loses momentum and falls to the ground.

"We spend our days as a tale that is told" (Psalm 90:9). Life is a composite of sentences, paragraphs, pages, chapters, and introduction and a conclusion. Need more be said?

Love is being able to do something for someone when he's not looking or when he will never even know who did it.

You can't sow the seed while the seed is still in the barn.

We need to remember constantly that what's up there is better than what's down here.

Some Things To Be Thankful For

- ▶ **Mom and Dad.** They gave you life.
- ▶ **Kids.** They teach you as much as you teach them.
- ▶ **Teachers.** They help you to know which is the right way to go.
- ▶ **Husband or Wife.** They know your weaknesses, your faults, your idiosyncracies, and love you anyway.
- ▶ **Detractors.** They make you take a good look at yourself.
- ▶ **A warm place to be.** But don't become so comfortable that you forget where you're going or what you have to do.

I Was Just Thinking...

There is more to sin than just making a mistake.

Life is more what you are than what you have.

Most of the time listening is more difficult than talking.

Meditation takes time—that's why many of us don't do it.

Tears are necessary sometimes—they wash out the bad stuff.

It's hard to be yourself when you don't really know who you are.

I Was Just Thinking... About Honesty

Honesty is relative in these days. Everyone agrees we need it, but nobody seems to know for sure what it is.

Actually, most people think honesty is whatever they think it is.

Some people apparently suppose honesty to be mathematical. Honesty is added in the case of the big, significant matters, but subtracted when it comes to the small matters.

Some folks seem to think honesty is situational—sometimes the situation calls for it, sometimes it doesn't.

Four Things To Consider Before You Decide

1. Will it inhibit my flight toward God?

2. Will it tend to tarnish my influence?

3. Will it edify or merely satisfy?

4. Will it stop there? And what if it doesn't?

—From That's Life, *p. 166*

Did I Say That?

I've been around some kind of recording equipment most of my life—first in broadcasting, then in making records in the music business, now with CDs, DVDs, jump drives, Cloud, etc., etc.

Have you ever listened to yourself on a recording of some kind? How'd you like it? How'd you sound? Were you surprised? How did your voice sound—smooth, raspy, squeeky, mellow? How were your pronunciations? Any drawl or colloquialisms? You sound like you thought you would?

> **God is recording every conversation.**

I have some news for you. God knows how you sound. He hears you. He knows what you say and to whom. He knows what prompted what you said in every situation. He is recording every conversation.

If you could hear what He hears, you might ask:

- "Did I say that?"
- "Did I say it like that?"
- "What was I thinking when I said that?"
- "Reckon anybody hear that?"

You might say:

- "I wish I hadn't said that."
- "I wish I hadn't said that like that."
- "I wish I could erase that.

"Behold, how great a matter a little fire kindeleth" (James 3:5)

Short Stops
"I love when I obey; I obey when I love."
—G. Campbell Morgan

Hope is our contact with eternity. It's sad when we lose it.

Sin is man's main malady.

Listening is more that just being quiet. Hearing more than just listening.

Truth
Everyone admits the need for truth. It suppresses ignorance, diminishes prejudice, eliminates superstition, alleviates undue pride. It encourages progress, promotes growth, enhances usefulness, and is basic to improvement. But truth is useless until it is supplied and applied.

All that's said in one simple statement: "Ye shall know the truth and the truth shall make you free." (John 8:32)

Artificial intelligence, so-called, is still just that—artificial. It cannot replicate the actions and emotions of the human soul.

My Prayer For Today
Lord, give me eyes to see above the world.
Lord, give me ears to hear truth.
Lord, give me hands to help.
Lord, give me feet to go where I need to go.
Lord, make my heart want to be like Him.

"The present time has one advantage over every other—it is our own."
—Charles Caleb Colton

"You can give without loving, but you can't love without giving."
—Amy Carmichael

I Was Just Thinking...

Sometimes I'm so interested in getting where I'm going that I fail to enjoy the trip.

Sometimes I get so taken up with my list that I fail to enjoy checking off each entry.

Sometimes I'm so careful to watch every step that I take my eye off the goal.

Sometimes my humility becomes a source for my pride.

Sometimes my effort to think before I speak becomes the reason for my not speaking at all.

Sometimes my loving criticism is not very lovely.

Sometimes when I think I know it already, it becomes a reason for not listening.

Sometimes I'm so busy looking at the faults of others that I don't see my own.

Sometimes my idea of balance is seriously slanted in my own direction.

Sometimes when I think I won, I actually lost.

Sometimes others don't view my successes the same way I do.

Sometimes my periods of relaxation are not relaxation at all, but periods of laziness.

Sometimes I want to get something done so I can start something not nearly as important as what I'm doing.

Sometimes my looking forward to tomorrow is merely an excuse for not finishing what I should have done today.

Sometimes my idea of toleration is little more than being afraid to speak.

Sometimes my work is unpleasant only because of my lack of appreciation for having work to do.

Can We?

Jesus was the friend of the poor, the help of the helpless, the bearer of the downtrodden. Can we be any less?

Jesus had time for the small, the insignificant, the ignorant, the uninformed, even the ill-informed. Can we do any less?

Jesus went about doing for those who couldn't do for themselves, lifting those who couldn't help themselves, teaching those who could not teach themselves. Can we do any less?

Jesus died for those who cursed Him, shed His blood for those who scourged Him, had mercy on those who were unmerciful, was nailed to a cross made of some of the wood He created; and after it was horribly done, He said, "Father, forgive them." Then He died for you and me. He could not do any less and save mankind. Can we not live for Him?

Two Thoughts Worth Thinking

"The beauty of woman must yield to the beauty of virtue."

"The rebellion of the body, sweet at the moment, only leads to trouble."
—Alexander the Great

Sketches

Life is not so much about what you get out of it, but what you give in it.

This life is not the end of matters. Man tends toward eternity. However, it is in this life and how it is lived that determines each man's eternal state. When this thing we call "life" is ended, man—each man—is propelled into eternity. Each man will spend eternity in one of two places—heaven, a place of unceasing bliss, or in hell, a place of horrible, never-ending torment. The joys of heaven are elegantly described in Scripture so as to entice us toward it. The horrors of hell are as sure as are the joys of heaven, and are graphically depicted in terms and figures intended to keep us far away for it. It thereby becomes an important question to ask: Where will you spend eternity?

Change and the future are inseparably connected.

To be ignorant is sad. To be wilfully ignorant is sadder yet.

To seek the elegant things in life is to get close to God.

Prayer is one of the first evidences of faith.

Seven Serious Excuses

1. " I don't think."
2. "I don't know."
3. "I don't care."
4. "I'm too busy."
5. " I leave well enough alone."
6. "I don't have time to read."
7. "I'm not interested."

What Prayer Does For Us

- ▶ Makes us like the thing adored.
- ▶ Exercises our spiritual senses.
- ▶ Humbles our elevated spirits.
- ▶ Elevates our broken spirits.
- ▶ Keeps us in touch with Him.

A Quick Look At the Attitudes

Note: There is no etymological connection between the words *attitude* and *beatitude*. They just sound akin. However, there is a connotation connection between the two words. Notice:

- ▶ "Blessed are the poor in spirit." An attitude of humility. Not proud.
- ▶ "Blessed are those that mourn." A sensitive attitude. Not unfeeling,
- ▶ "Blessed are the meek." A gentle attitude. Not controlling.
- ▶ "Blessed are those who hunger and thirst after righteousness." A reasonable attitude. Seeking right courses to pursue.
- ▶ "Blessed are the merciful." A compassionate attitude. An abiding care for what happens.
- ▶ "Blessed are the pure in heart." A clear perspective, or a clean mental attitude. Not prejudicial.
- ▶ "Blessed are the peacemakers." An agreeable attitude. Not disposed to unnecessary controversy.
- ▶ "Blessed are those who are persecuted for righteousness sake." A determined attitude. Not vindictive.

Things I Have Read

"To love is to be vulnerable. Love anything, and your heart will certainly be wrung and possibly be broken. If you want to make sure of keeping it intact, you must give your heart to no one. Wrap it carefully round with hobbies and little luxuries; avoid all entanglements; lock it up safe in the casket or coffin of your selfishness. And in that casket of selfishness your heart begins to change. It becomes hard, unbreakable, irredeemable. The only place outside of Heaven where you can be perfectly safe from all the dangers of love is Hell."
—C. S. Lewis, *The Four Loves*

"You have lost your religion if you have lost your love."
—*G. Campbell Morgan*

"When I pity me—
   And count my burdens, one by one,"
   My thoughts become a grey
   That blankets faith, and hope, and love;
   And casts dark shadows in my way.
   The friendly word that's given to cheer
   Is smothered by a faithless fear,
   And sinks into a hopeless sea;
   When I pity me."
—*Robert F. Turner,* What It Is, Is Preaching

Some Journal Notes

"A man is seldom more pompous than when he refuses to hear."

"Today is Wednesday—I think."

Snippets

In the final reality, I go where I choose to go.

So often, to lose your temper is to lose the battle.

Most people want little more than to be noticed and to be somewhat appreciated.

An honest person is one who will listen, even if he disagrees.

All my potential and possibilities are determined by my will to use them.

Journal Notes

"Fall is upon us. Coming tonight, supposedly. Sweater weather? Can it be for away? I like it."

"Yesterday was good. Work was easy, labor was sweet."

"I struggled somewhat with my sermon yesterday. I just was not very sharp mentally. It sometimes doesn't come easy. Mental constipation, I suppose."

"Yesterday I dropped nearly everything I picked up. Some days are just like that."

"After all that, I fall short."

"I was just thinking today as I plodded along: I am who I am. I am what I am. I am where I am. So I need to manage these three facts of the matter. And, with God's help, I shall."

I Was Just Thinking...

You can't do much about a problem until you first admit that it exists.

You can't press on toward the goal while you're looking the other way.

To defer to do good is to defer to be good.

You can't believe in Jesus until you believe all that He said.

It's wise to stop once in a while and take a look at the little things. They matter.

To a true servant of God, "Do I have to be there on Wednesday night?" is like a young boy asking, "Do I have to eat this homemade ice cream?"

Doing it today, even if it's inconvenient, is better than regretting not having done it tomorrow.

A happy family is a gift from God.

That reminds me of a statement made by Leo Tolstoy: "All happy families resemble one another, but each unhappy family is unhappy in its own way."

There's more to worship than just being there. There has to be a self-presentation made to God before there is any worship.

Prayer keeps you close to God. Neglect it and you will drift away.

Far too many people spend time, effort, and money for a "makeover," but don't have time to "make-over" the part of them that really matters.

Some Pertinent Paragraphs

Man, left unattended by inspiration, stands confused, bewildered, perplexed, confounded. He finds great exasperation in his efforts to explain himself—what is his purpose in life, what is his eventuality. Furthermore, he is confused as to truth and his relationship toward it. But he has Jesus, who came to relieve his consternation, release him from his superstitions, take away his fears, and identify for him a right course to pursue. Thank God, Jesus has lifted us!

In this age there is a constant bombardment of the mind by the devil. He is seeking a place to stay. The competition for the mind is relentless and subtle. Secularism is cleverly disguised as success; materialism wears the mask of excellence; free love is passed off as freedom of human expression; homosexuality is identified as an alternate life style. The answer to his constant effort to control us is simple: "Give no place to the devil."

> **Thank God, Jesus has lifted us!**

Winston Churchill, in an address at Harvard University in 1943, said, almost prophetically, "The empires of the future will be empires of the mind." He was right. In fact, man has in his own mind elevated himself to a height that makes him equal to, if not greater than God—assuming he still believes there is a God. As a result of this contemporary reasoning, religion in general has degenerated in our age to a rather pitiful version of what it once was. This transition has produced a kind of religious conglomeration of human philosophy, a Darwinistic opinion that pompously proposes that man is little more than a talented animal, and that no truth exists outside of man—a sort of subjective conclusion that says everyone is OK, no matter what he is or what he believes. So there's no need to worry about the Bible or religion, or going to worship services in today's world. Religion today seems to me to have concluded that God did not create man, man created God.

Final Points To Ponder
If you're not getting better, you're likely getting worse.

To walk is to proceed one step at a time.

Gradual growth is the healthiest kind.

Personal pondering usually proceeds from a private location.

Little True-isms
Fundamentals are necessary to any success.

It is not ours to question, but to obey.

Sin is far more dangerous than Ebola and yet it receives little notice.

You can't get there by just dreaming about your arrival.

One of David's problems? He stayed too long at the "sight," or is it "site"?

Value
Value is measured not by what it will buy, but what it can contribute. For instance:

- True love is more valuable than erotica.
- Honesty is more valuable than winning.
- Character is more valuable than reputation.
- Bondage is more valuable than freedom without truth.
- The hereafter is more valuable than the here.

The Value of the Claims of Jesus

- "I am the bread of life" (John 6:35). We need spiritual sustenance.
- "I am the light of the world" (John 8:12). We need spiritual illumination.
- "I am the way, the truth, and the life" (John 14:6). We need a high way.
- "I am the door of the sheep" (John 10:7–9). We need access.
- "I am the good shepherd" (John 10:11–14). We need guidance.
- "I am the vine" (John 15:1–8). We need a divine connection.
- "I am the resurrection and the life" (John 11:25–26). We need resurrection.

A Poem To Remember

We search the world for truth; we cull
The good, the pure, the beautiful,
From graven and written scroll,
From all old flower fields of the soul;
And weary seekers of the best,
We come back laden from our quest
To find that all the sages said
Is in the book our mothers read.

—*John Greenleaf Whittier*

The Value of True Love (1 Corinthians 13)

True love:

- "Suffers long." There is great value in being patient, staying in your place and waiting.
- "Is kind." Who can measure the value of one simple act of kindness.
- "Envieth not." There is value in acknowledging the talents of others.
- "Vaunteth not itself." A person's value is seldom measured by how he measures himself.
- "Is not puffed up." Self-inflation is valueless pomposity.
- "Doth not behave itself unseemly." There is much value in appropriate behavior.
- "Is not easily provoked." That person who controls himself in times of difficulty is of considerable value to whatever the situation.
- "Thinketh no evil." Who can measure the worth of a clean, unbiased mind?
- "Beareth, believeth, hopeth, endureth all things." Here is a sum total of the attributes of love, added together. How valuable they are!

Joseph—Man of God

Joseph is one of the most interesting characters in the Bible. His life was exemplary, his attitudes and character worthy of emulation.

- He was kind (Genesis 40:7–8).
- He was humble (Genesis 41:16; 45:7–9).
- He was wise (Genesis 41:33–57).
- He had great faith (Genesis 45:5–8).

Snippets
The hardest reading of all is reading between the lines.

Nobody is conceited. If you don't believe it, just ask him.

Don't be to quick to judge; you may become guilty.

"By failing to prepare, you are preparing to fail."
—Benjamin Franklin

Anger stirred, becomes wrath; wrath stirred, becomes malice; malice stirred becomes bitterness.

No person ever becomes suddenly bitter; it takes time—you have to cook it slowly.

Indifference often comes out of affluence.

It is not time for satisfaction. We're not there yet.

It's hard to hear when your mouth is open.

Shorties
Work is not nearly as imposing if the goal is in sight.

Life is a matter of looking out, looking around, looking up, and giving only slight attention to looking back.

Time marches on with little or no regard for what happens as it goes.

You can always find some dirt if you're looking for it.

Journal Notes

"It occurs to me that a preacher must approach his life with a degree of confidence, but without pomposity; not with superiority, but as one with the people. It fact, I suppose that to be a good course of pursuit for everyone."

"What a blessing it is to have brethren at your side. They make the difficult times easier to bear and share the joy when times are good."

"It's interesting to me when you stop and think about it: we'll spend extra hours at the gym in an effort to keep our physical bodies in good shape, but only a minimal amount of time in an effort to care for our spiritual being. Which one do we suppose will last longer?"

"I have to work some tomorrow on my column. My creativity is not at a very high level right now. But, as I've often remarked, 'there's this strange connection between inspiration and deadlines.' It is not time to rest."

"In my opinion, meditation is fast becoming a lost art. Our thinking today is dominated by external observations, leaving little time for internal reflections."

"The Bible is about people—all kinds of people—each with a lesson for those who take the time to read it."

What It Takes To Stand
A firm foundation
A commitment to stay put
A willingness to hurt some
A long range focus

What It Takes To Fall
A poor footing
A short vision
A nominal persuasion
A short attention span

Now, you apply the passages and you have a sermon—one for you and one for another.

All About Anger
No matter how true it is or how you say it, if there's no love in it, it won't be very readily received.

According to the Scriptures, you have only about 12 hours to tolerate anger (Ephesians 4:26).

One good way to prevent anger: Would I want that said to me? And would I want it said that way?

There's usually a good amount of pride before there's anger.

He who is constantly looking for faults in others seldom looks at himself.

There is yet a place for righteous indignation—being angry about failure, about invasions of impurity, being disgusted with the flesh.

There is an old Slovakian proverb which says, "Anger is the only thing to put off till tomorrow."

Aristotle may have had it right when he averred that meekness is the mean between extreme anger and extreme angerlessness.

Anger usually has in it at least a moderate amount of agitation. The word *agitate* comes from Middle English and originally meant "to drive away." Need more be said?

Snippets

A good education is based on truth, not speculation.

Be yourself! You can't actually be anybody else anyway.

Life changes. Get used to it.

Holding a grudge is like having a constant stomach ache.

"Behold thyself." That's hard. We kind of have the mirror fixed so that it reflects not what we are, but what we want to see.

It's never too late to start over.

The Practical Side of the Beatitudes

"Blessed are the poor in spirit." They will acknowledge the King in their hearts. That's what blessedness is all about.

"Blessed are those that mourn." They will find a place for comfort and consolation in the kingdom.

"Blessed are the meek." They will find way to God through a spirit of total submission and commitment to Him.

"Blessed are those who hunger and thirst after righteousness." Their appetite for the right things will be satisfied. They will be filled.

"Blessed are the merciful." They will have the joy of reaping for themselves the mercy they have given to others.

"Blessed are the pure in heart." Physical sight sees only physical things. Faith can see past here, see God.

"Blessed are the peacemakers." What an honor to hear it said, "you look like your Father."

"Blessed are the persecuted." Kingdom-lovers will suffer—but willingly—for the kingdom of God is the main focus in his life.

Ventings

From all that I hear, *50 Shades of Grey* is not grey at all, it's black—disgustingly, dirty black!

It seems to me that we are immersed in a cult of youth in this age. Is it wrong to be old? To look old? To act old? I hope not.

If you're too busy to take ten minutes out and pray to God, you're too busy.

If all you're giving to God is money, something's wrong in your life.

It's very often easier to speak than to listen. Listening is a sign of personal control and can be a rich experience if we but learn to do so.

If we spent as much time adorning our soul as we do adorning our visage, we might not be better looking, but we'd be better.

> **If you're too busy to take ten minutes to pray, you're too busy.**

Short Stops

We would do well to stop complaining and start working.

We would do well to stop the gossip as soon as it get to us.

We would do well to stop at the stop signs and go when He says go.

We would do well to stop and take a deep breath now and then.

We would do well to stop letting bad things penetrate our thinking.

We would do well to force pride out and let humility in.

We would do well to stop and think before we quit too early.

Observations

It only takes a moment and a simple small compliment to give someone a quick boost.

In fact, a word of encouragement can often give a better boost than those energy drinks.

Sympathy, it seems to me, is more than just feeling sorry for someone, but feeling sorry *with* someone.

Life is a story. We write it a bit at a time. It behooves us to write carefully—and to erase, by the grace of God, the bad stuff we sometimes write.

Pessimism seldom helps anything. It retards energy and blunts progress.

In that connection, I read where Paul Harvey once said, "I've never seen a monument erected to a pessimist." Me neither.

The only way to be truly happy is to be at peace with God.

It's not wrong to cry. Sometimes we need to cry. It flushes out the bad stuff. And, sometimes tears are our tenderest and best expressions of true joy.

Love is the divine motive. It energizes good things. Love is the divine mucilage. It binds all the good things together.

Go and visit a sick person. I guarantee you'll take away more than you gave.

The Scriptures are not profitable to those who make no investment in them.

"We're just looking for them who are looking for Him."
—Ed Harrell

Time is for man; man is for time. We had better use it well while some of it is still ours.

Short Stops

"Love you" loses part of its force when you leave the "I" out of it.

You have to figure out where you are before you can get where you're going.

If you can't thank God for it, you better not do it.

Life is just like the weather—it changes every day.

How would you live your life if you knew exactly how much of it you had?

The true quality life is not material, it's spiritual.

The person who flaunts his talent flouts the law of humility (Proverbs 16:18–19).

One-way Street

Jesus said, "I am the way, the truth and the life." If we would go where we ought to go, it will be by His guidance, for He said, "No man cometh to the Father, but by me."

Journal Notes

It is the grand privilege of man to reflect the glory of his Creator. It is in His image that man was created, and only when he reflects that image as nearly as possible does he fulfill his real purpose in life" (1 Corinthians 1:29).

Purity is an advantage, no matter the project or enterprise. It takes away what would otherwise impede the progress of that enterprise (Matthew 5:8).

To spend no time with God is to show a want of sense and, worse still, a spirit of ingratitude (1 Thessalonians 5:17).

Life is more than just living. Life is meant for service—service to Him who gave it, service to those who have it. It will never satisfy until it is lived as it was meant to be (Psalm 16:11).

What we want and what we need are often not the same. The reason is simple: we don't always know what we need. Is that not reason enough to ask our Father for help? (Philippians 4:19).

When Life Gets Wearisome, Remember Where You're Going

When the road seems long and every turn is hard, when it's a struggle to continually go on, and there's nobody near to cheer you along, Remember where you're going.

When the loads of life are heavy, when its burdens keep shifting, and when breath is hard to get, Remember where you're going.

When progress seem slow, when you take two steps only to fall back one, and it would seem to be easier to quit, Remember where you're going.

When the end seems so far away and the path keeps getting harder with so many hills yet to climb, each one steeper than the last, Remember where you're going.

When you find that getting closer doesn't make it any easier, and when you're in sight of the end and the last mile seems to be the most difficult, Remember where you're going.

When you finally get there, when you've crossed the finish line and you look back at the trail with all its difficulties, when you can finally take a deep breath and realize it's over, you will look back at what made you keep on. You remembered where you were going.

Sketches

Anxiety is composed of two basic parts: fear and anticipation. It ranges from abject fear to a happy anticipation of good, from worry to simple uneasiness. It's sometimes very intense, sometimes not so much so.

We have some of it most every day. It permeates our lives in ways that are sometimes predictable sometimes not, but it's always around.

Remember how it was at test time? Well, that's just as true when you have hospital tests. Remember how it was on your first date? Well, that's just how it is again when your kids have their first date.

Most of us learn how to regulate our anxiety, but that's certainly no indication that we have controlled it. It'll be back pretty soon in some form or the other.

Handling anxiety—in all its various forms—is accomplished by faith. Faith eases. Faith erases worry and quiets fear by the assurance of good things to come.

Short Sermons
Watch Out! (1 Thessalonians 5:6)

   I. **A lamentable fact: "some sleep"**
      A. The disinterested world
      B. The indifferent Christian

  II. **A stern warning: "let us not sleep"**
      A. We know better
      B. We are reflectors of light

 III. **A remedy offered: "watch"**
      A. Look where you're going
      B. Danger of worldly inebriants
      C. Equip yourself

—*From* Just A Minute

I Was Just Thinking...

Endurance is the ability to hold on when the wind's blowing in your face.

From my journal: I need to be more aware that our word *kind* and *kin* are *kindred* terms.

Motor and *motivation* are akin. A motor drives a vehicle; motive drives our selves. We need more moter-vation.

And was it not Zig Ziglar who said, "People often say that motivation doesn't last. Well, neither does bathing—that's why we recommend it daily."

Intelligence is not just knowing something, it's knowing how that something works for the good of others.

How often we pray for the things we want and leave undone prayers for things we need.

"Forgive" carries with it the idea of sending away. Aren't we grateful that God gives away our sins, never allowing them to return?

Dangers In Neglect

- ▶ We have neglected our salvation when we do not radiate the love of God in our lives (1 John 4:7–11).
- ▶ We have neglected our salvation when we are indifferent to the needs of lost souls (Romans 1:14–15)
- ▶ We have neglected our salvation when we have lost a burning desire to improve (Ephesians 4:11–16).
- ▶ We have neglected our salvation when we leave God out of our choices (Matthew 6:24).

Post Scripts

No matter how busy you are, remember to take a few minutes and pray.

No matter how the situation looks right now, remember to pray.

When all's going well, remember to thank God for it.

Remember to pray for opportunities to bring someone to Him.

A good way to get the day started is to remember to pray.

BE WISE SMALL

Index

The Ageless Nature Of God's Word 36
All About Anger 97
Be Careful! 4
Be Wise Small 32
Be Wise Small Bits 80
Be Wise Small Snippets 66
Be Wise Small Suggestions 56
Be Wise Small—But Watch Out! 7
Be Wise Small-isms 16
Best Be Careful! 79
Books Worth a Read 59
Can We? 85
A Challenge 40
Concern For Concern 17
Dangers In Neglect 105
Did I Say That? 82
"Examine Yourself" (2 Corinthians 13:5) 17
Facts vs. Fiction 41
A Few Pertinent Questions 15

INDEX

Final Points To Ponder 92
For the New Year 39
Forgiveness 36
Four Things To Consider Before You Decide. 81
Four Ways To Make a Good Day Even Better. 64
From My Journal 9, 44, 51, 65
From Other Sources 3
Give Thanks Today 3
Hold Hands 4
Hope 30
How To Have A Good Day 38
Humility 18
I Don't Know Why 64
I Was Just Thinking 10, 44, 70, 81, 84, 90, 104
I Was Just Thinking…About Honesty. 81
I-ddiction. 72
Jesus Was Real 43
Joseph—Man of God 94
Journal Notes 89
Journal Notes 96
Journal Notes 102
Jump Starters 43
Just a Couple of Things 28
Just a Little 6

INDEX

Just a Word or Two 51
Leftovers 10, 25, 71
Letters: What Would I Write? 24
Listen a Little 26
A Little More 7
Little Things Mean a Lot 15
The Little Tree In The Gutter: A Parable 34
Little True-isms 92
Look at This 42
My Heroes 12, 28
My Prayer For Today 83
Natural vs. Unnatural Disasters 53
Observations 100
One-way Street 101
Paragraphical Ponderings 60
Part-Time Christians 15
Permitted Plagiarism 20
Personality Considerations For Private Moments 69
A Poem To Remember 93
Post Scripts 105
The Practical Side of the Beatitudes 98
Prayer 46
A Psalm 41
A Quick Look At the Attitudes 87

INDEX

Remember Where You're Going 102
R. J. Stevens: Who He Really Was. 39
The Rope of Hope 26
Sermon Outline 65
Seven Serious Excuses. 86
A Short Sermon 22
Short Sermons 104
Short Stops 5, 10, 28, 30, 45, 72, 83, 99, 101
Short Stuff 21, 25
Shorties 95
Silent Speech. 8
The Simplicity of God's Plan: 52
Sketches. 86
Sketches. 103
Small Bits 19
Small Pieces 6
A Small Prayer 14
A Small Sermon 6
Small Stuff From a Fellow's Journal. 18
Small Thoughts I Had Today. 2
Snippets. 30, 33, 37, 40, 44, 50, 56, 59, 76, 89, 95, 98
Some Great Men of God 11
Some Journal Notes. 88
Some Little Things We All Can Do 24

INDEX

Some Pertinent Paragraphs 91
Some Short Journal Entries 50
Some Small Thoughts About Words 23
Some Things To Be Thankful For 80
Some Things We Can Learn From .61
   David's Encounter With Goliath
Some Thoughts From My Journal 5
Some Thoughts on Colossians 1:9–11 12
Someone Said 52
Stuff I See 66
Sunday Morning Starters 79
Sunday Starters 33
Take a Few Minutes Today and 56
Take Time To Be Holy 42
Take Time To Love 76
Ten Short Paragraphs for Your Marriage 12
That Peer Pressure 58
Things I Have Read 88
Things I Think I Can Do Better 49
Things My Daddy Told Me 1
Things You Should Tell Your Children 61
Truth 83
Two Thoughts Worth Thinking 85
Value 92

INDEX

The Value of the Claims of Jesus 93
The Value of True Love (1 Corinthians 13) 94
Ventings 99
Wanna Have A Good Day? 32
What Ever Happened? 16
What It Takes To Fall 97
What It Takes To Stand 96
What Prayer Does For Us 87
What Truth Is… 37
What Work Does 37
When Life Gets Wearisome, ...102
   Remember Where You're Going
Word of the Month Club 58
Word Pictures 45
Worship 76
www.warning.com 46
Yes, I Can! 35
Your Own Back Yard 8

CPSIA information can be obtained
at www.ICGtesting.com
Printed in the USA
LVOW01s2335020216
473447LV00002B/2/P